3/6/02

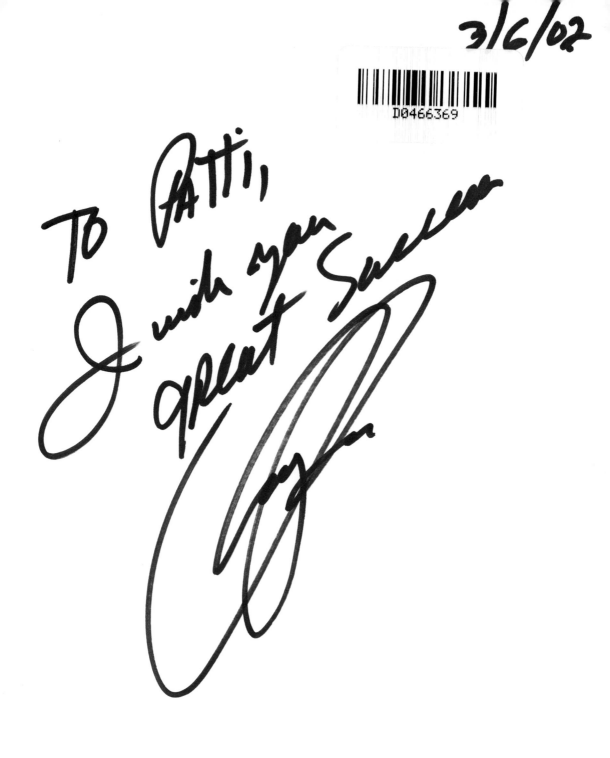

TO Patti,
I wish you
great Success

What Leaders Are Saying About Omar Periu's Book
From Management to Leadership...

"*From Management to Leadership* provides the reader with some concrete ideas on how to become a more effective leader. It is easy to lead when the going is good. How to overcome adversity and complacency require different tactics. This book helps the good manager become a great manager, the average manager to become a good manager and a beginning manager to become an effective one.

You hit the important points to developing true leaders. Trust and confidence, attitude and motivation are not just words, they are tools to effective management. I know that this book is going to be a success. It has all the ingredients of a winner.

> Lou Holtz, Head Football Coach
> University of South Carolina

"Omar Periu is among the top management speakers and trainers in the US today. His fast-moving book, *From Management to Leadership* is full of helpful, practical, immediately applicable ideas and information that anyone can use to get better results immediately."

> Brian Tracy, President,
> Brian Tracy International

"WOW! The definitive manual on the path to becoming a successful leader. Omar should know...he has been instrumental in our company's growth from 400 to over 2,000 people in the six years since we met."

> Joe Walsh, CEO
> Yellow Book USA

"The business world is constantly changing, and how you lead your people will greatly determine your organization's success. Our approach must be that of leading a team instead of merely managing employees. Omar Periu's book is a helpful tool for bridging this gap. *From Management to Leadership* is a must have for every leader's personal library.

> John C. Maxwell, Founder
> The INJOY Group

"I wish we could put a Chicken Soup For The Soul cover on this book. It is destined to go to the top. Omar Periu is a real professional. I consider him among the top trainers in the world..."

> Mark Victor Hansen, Co-Author of *Chicken Soup For The Soul*,
> Co-Founder of the 3% Club

"Whether you're in charge of a small business or a growing corporation, you face the everyday challenges of leadership. Omar Periu gives you the most practical, hands-on, how-to leadership skills ever written. Invest in this book."

> Ken Summers, CEO
> One Valley Bank

"Omar Periu delivers an excellent book that deserves to be read from cover to cover or as a survival guide to successful leadership. All leaders and managers in our highly competitive and ever changing business climate should read this book."

Peter Lowe, CEO
Success Events International

"In this book, Omar Periu combines his hands-on, street smart knowledge with the head smart skills of leadership. A must read book for anyone who is in the leadership position."

Jim Piccolo, President & CEO
Tru-Dynamics, Inc.

"Managing a sales force is quite different from any other type of management experience. Within these pages, you, Mr. or Ms. Sales Manager, will find a wealth of information to help you develop a successful sales team."

Tom Hopkins, Master Sales Trainer
Author of *How to Master the Art of Selling*

"Omar Periu is today's top trainer in sales and sales management. This book gives you the tools and concepts to be a successful manager in any industry. Most importantly, as you read this book you will gain ideas you can put into action immediately...This is not a book on theory--it tells you how to do it! Each chapter will give you tools you can put to work immediately."

Scott Patterson, CEO
Trinity Holdings, Inc.

"When it comes to Selling, Sales Management and Leadership in the sales profession, Omar Periu is the person I recommend to all of my clients. Before Omar's materials, the sales and leadership process was long and never ending. Today's marketplace has changed. Omar Periu's book, *From Management to Leadership*, is what is needed in today's marketplace to have the competitive advantage. You're going to love the tools you'll receive from this book!"

Bob Proctor, Author of *Born Rich*,
Co-Founder of the 3% Club

"When you implement the leadership secrets in this book, you will make a tremendous difference in your effectiveness, your life and the lives of those around you."

Tom Vaught, Vice President,
Fitness USA Supercenters

Omar managed one of our divisions for over a decade with Tom Hopkins International, as well as taught sales management to thousands of our clients. His message is current and vital, coming from years of hands-on experience in the industry. I have had the privilege to work with Omar for over 20 years, and his unparalleled success record with national and international leaders and managers will make this book an invaluable resource.

Tom Murphy, Co-founder of Tom Hopkins International
Author of *Premeditated Success*

FROM
MANAGEMENT
TO
LEADERSHIP

How to Out Think,
Out Perform and
Out Produce the Competition

by
Omar Periu

Omar Periu
INTERNATIONAL™

From Management to Leadership

Published by
Omar Periu International, Inc.
P.O. Box 812470
Boca Raton, FL   33481
www.OmarPeriu.com

Library of Congress Cataloging-in-Publication Data
available upon request

ISBN: 0-9704368-0-7

Printed in the United States of America

First Edition

For sales inquiries and special prices for bulk quantities, please contact Omar Periu International, Inc. at 888-777-4519 or write to the address in the back of this book.

ABOUT OMAR PERIU

Omar Periu is a powerful man with a truly remarkable life story. He's more than a motivator; his peers refer to him as *"The Motivational Teacher."* Possessing an indefinable quality of magnetism, Omar's educational seminars raise audience awareness to a higher level. Although the terms *"dynamic," "high energy"* and *"super achiever"* all describe Omar Periu as he is today, they aren't exactly the words that portrayed the results accomplished earlier in his career.

Omar and his family fled Castro's regime when he was only seven years old. They arrived in Miami with no money, no relatives or friends in America and nothing but the clothes on their backs. Thus began Omar's journey of success in the land of freedom and opportunity.

Enduring the taunting of other children, the cold winters of Illinois and the language barrier, Omar made a conscious and deliberate decision to pursuit his dream of personal achievement. His father, reading from a tattered Spanish copy of Dale Carnegie's book, *"How To Win Friends and Influence People,"* taught Omar one of the greatest lessons in life. *"It doesn't matter who you are, where you're from or what color you are, you can do anything you put your mind to."*

Initially, Omar had a limited understanding and little success with the sales and leadership process and its outcome. However, after studying the masters and observing the difference between the performance of top salespeople and successful entrepreneurs compared to those barely squeaking by, Omar developed *The Investigative Selling Principles.* Implementing those investigative principles in his own career, it wasn't long before Omar became one of the top professionals in his field. Before the age of 31, he was a self-made multi-millionaire, owning some of the most profitable health clubs and sports medicine facilities in the United States. From his modest beginnings as a take-it-on-the-chin salesperson, Omar knew the pain of sales rejection and failure. He also discovered the high of mastering sales presentations and sophisticated closing skills. Most importantly, he is now teaching these unique investigative principles to salespeople, managers and entrepreneurs all over the world. Like Omar's experience, having internalized these principles, his students are now reporting their greatest sales triumphs ever!

His tremendous success led him into sales management, and he has devoted the last 20 years to the training and development of sales and leadership professionals. Since that time, Omar has provided high-impact instruction on the topic of sales management and sales leadership throughout the world with live seminars, cassettes, CD's, coaching, mentoring and in-house video training systems.

He has personally recruited, hired, trained and managed both inside telephone-based sales associates and retail/field salespeople, as well as customer service professionals. Furthermore, since sales leadership is an ever-changing discipline; he felt it was imperative that he kept his finger on the pulse by currently managing his own corporations and sales professionals on a daily basis. This hands-on, in-the-trenches sales and sales management leadership has made Omar one of the top sales management and leadership trainers in the world.

Omar's content is fresh and inspiring, his presentations impeccable, and his story unforgettable. He is now referred to as the number one "how to" sales and leadership trainer in America, a world-traveled speaker who has spent over a decade educating salespeople, managers and entrepreneurs worldwide. He has trained more than two million people in more than two-thirds of the Fortune 500 companies, teaching over 5,000 seminars, workshops and training programs in his career. He is a member of The National Speakers Association and has been inducted into the prestigious International Platform Association.

Through hard work and determination, Omar became recognized as a highly professional salesperson, sales leader and entrepreneur. You can do the same. He is committed to helping people like you achieve their full potential through mastering *"The Investigative Selling Principles"* and his outstanding *"Success Strategies,"* and now this new, exciting book *"From Management to Leadership."* To quote Omar's philosophy—*"Success is in the moment—so make each moment count!"*

DEDICATION

This book is dedicated to my wife, Helen, who is a living example of generosity, unconditional love and support. Thank you for encouraging and inspiring me to live my dream, which is to help others achieve greatness.

ACKNOWLEDGEMENTS

❖ I must first recognize my wonderful wife, Helen. I am grateful for your patience and understanding when my life's calling takes me away.

❖ A special appreciation to my mother and father for their endless support and lifetime of encouragement. My path to success was cleared by their examples of great leadership

❖ I would also like to thank Debi Siegel for her outstanding, creative writing talents. It's great to have someone so dedicated, hard working and professional to count on to take the project from beginning to end.

❖ A special thanks to Doug Siegel for his countless hours working on the layout and cover design that would creatively surround my words and present them in an easy to read and remember design.

❖ It would be remiss of me if I failed to thank all my teachers and mentors who participated in my educational experience—both personally and professionally. I am who I am today because of the time you invested in my development.

❖ Last but not least, thanks to you, the reader. Thank goodness there are people like you who are willing to do the work to progress from managers to highly successful, future leaders.

I Wish You Great Success!

FOREWORD

Omar Periu's book, *From Management to Leadership*, covers the waterfront in a very significant way. It's chock full of how-to's, and along the way we also learn why things should be done. That's important because people who know what to do and how to do it, then do it, will always have a job; those who know *why* it needs to be done will be the managers and ultimately the leaders.

Omar has definitely broken some new ground as he lays out his ideas, concepts and procedures. This is a book you will enjoy reading, but of infinitely more importance, you will appreciate and benefit from the lessons and procedures that he covers. You will also discover that when you carefully mark the areas in which you display certain strengths and weaknesses so that you can more easily pinpoint them in your second and third readings, your benefits will continue to grow. I mention this because it's important that you read this book first, mark it appropriately, and then study it. Keep it on hand as a reference book.

A study at Stanford University revealed that 95% of people who buy an idea do not follow through simply because they do not have the resources. In your first reading of *From Management to Leadership* you will buy the idea; then by keeping the book handy you will have the resources necessary to fulfill your objective of becoming a leader.

I'd like to emphasize that there is no such thing as a "born manager" or a "born leader." At least I've never read a notice in the newspaper where a couple has given birth to a manager or leader. But I frequently see in the obituary column where managers and leaders die, so obviously somewhere in between birth and death they achieved those positions if they took the proper steps. This book provides the direction so that you can be a more effective manager and, ultimately, the leader you desire to become. One prerequisite for this is that you learn to manage yourself and in the process you will learn to lead others.

Zig Ziglar

HELPFUL ICONS

 Indicates the position taken by peak-performing sales managers.

 Indicates training tips on how to become a top sales manager.

 Indicates very important quotes or words of wisdom--listen carefully.

 Indicates very important statements, ideas or concepts today's leaders don't want to forget.

 Indicates a warning or negative behavior that runs contrary to those practiced by top sales managers.

Contents

CHAPTER ONE

I Dared to Dream

"Always dream and shoot higher than you know you can do. Don't bother just to be better than your contemporaries or predecessors. Try to be better than yourself."

Old Chinese Proverb

Chapter Highlights:

▶ The Transformation from Management to Leadership

▶ Adopting the NEVER GIVE UP Management Philosophy

▶ Omar's Personal Journey to Effective Leadership

▶ Creating A Superior Sales Team

▶ Relating Your Own Management Story

▶ How Will This Book Help You?

▶ Visualize Becoming A Successful Manager

While every form of business management is challenging, our research shows that the management or leadership of salespeople is certainly one of the most dynamic and difficult of all disciplines. For over 20 years, I've dedicated my life to transforming managers into leaders and have witnessed the long-term benefits when a leader's cycle of personal growth and professional achievement spirals higher than he or she ever dreamed possible.

Unfortunately, I've also seen the results when companies put more faith in the strength of their advertising campaign than that of their managers. I personally believe that nothing takes the place of well-trained sales managers and their ability to lead their sales team by providing ongoing education opportunities and proven skill-building strategies. Visionary leaders not only understand the increased profits that success brings, but they also realize its liberating empowerment.

> That's my goal in all my seminars, custom workshops and personally researched and developed training materials—to transform managers into leaders. No great sales manager was born great. He or she was trained to be great— educated by someone whose inspiration created a desire to DO more, BE more and HAVE more.

Fortunately, I too learned from those types of leaders because I actively sought them out, questioned, listened and implemented their proven techniques. I listened and applied those leaders' expertise to my career and coupled their knowledge with my experience to create a program that has evolved into one of the most practical, hands-on, in-the-trenches, high-impact instructional tools in the industry. For over a decade, I've had the privilege of training over two-thirds of the Fortune 500 company leaders in over 2,500 seminars presented all over the world.

Although incredibly rewarding, I wish I could say the journey from management to leadership was always easy and enjoyable. Truth is, I've experienced the same challenges you may be going through right now with your salespeople, your company and even yourself. I truly understand your position as manager. I have been out in the field knocking on doors with my salespeople. I've sat for hours completing mountains of tedious paperwork to satisfy quarterly quota reports. And, I've attended hundreds of "so-called" educational seminars that did little more than offer temporary hype or recognize the problems I was experiencing without offering viable solutions.

Sometimes it's a good thing we don't know what the future will bring or we might fade before the finish.

> My road to successful management was littered with detours and potholes, but, over the years, I embraced the same philosophy as highly effective leaders—NEVER GIVE UP!

This belief or philosophy had much to do with my upbringing, so let me share with you my story.

My Story

I was only a small child when my family escaped Communist Cuba to come to America—the land of opportunity. Even when times were tough, I never stopped thinking that America would be the land of opportunity for me. There were times when the kids would make fun of me at school because I couldn't speak the language or because I didn't have the best clothes. During the tough times, it didn't seem like I had as good a chance to make it as the next guy. Often times, things just didn't feel equal. However, every time I was feeling low, my mom and dad would be there to encourage me, to tell me I could do anything now that I was in America. I was so fortunate to have been blessed with such great parents.

How could they have known what I would become? Sometimes parents just know those things, I guess. They are able to see greatness where others' vision is clouded by the child's immature behavior or foolish ideas. That describes me—immature and foolish, but beneath it all my parents recognized the strong character they had helped to instill in me.

> They were building a leader, and they expected me to achieve. I'm living proof that what you expect you usually get!

Who would have thought I'd be teaching hundreds of thousands of managers how to lead their people? Who would have guessed that a seven-year-old immigrant from Cuba would lead American businessmen and women to greater levels of success than they ever thought possible?

Who would have? I'll tell you—my mother and father—that's who. I was quite fortunate to have a father who understood the importance of studying great leaders. He also made sure I was exposed to greatness at an early age. And I learned from my father who shared with me the words of Dale Carnegie: "Feeling sorry for yourself, and your present condition, is not only a waste of energy but the worst habit you could possibly have." Not to mention a mother who all her life called me, "Me Rey," which means—"Little King."

My parents saw something in me that I didn't see in myself for quite some time. When I think of the ways they always challenged me to be my best and believed that I would rise to the occasion, I'm reminded of a speech my mentor once shared with me that was delivered by one of his teachers:

"You have greatness within you—something special. If just one of you can get a glimpse of a larger vision of yourself, of who you really are, of what it is you were meant to contribute, then the world will never be the same again. Be proud! You have within you the ability to touch millions of people's lives."

I didn't discover until many years later that those words weren't just for the especially gifted or wealthy. They applied to all who ever felt incapable of achievement, to those who experienced low self-esteem and were at times unable to reach their full potential because they were held back by that inner voice that shouted in their heads, "Who are you kidding? You will never be a success."

It's no wonder I didn't see leadership material in myself when I was living in a one-room apartment in Los Angeles making $147 per month as a struggling salesperson. I didn't see myself becoming a young entrepreneur and multi-millionaire by the time I was 31 years old, when at the time my meals consisted of tuna in the can. Upon first entered the selling arena, all I could see were overwhelming hardships and endless disappointments.

Then I decided to follow my parents' advice and believe in myself—invest in myself—much like some of you have invested in yourselves by purchasing this book. I met a man named Tom Murphy, who later became my mentor, and I soaked up every bit of wisdom he had to give. After casually mentioning a book he found interesting, I'd run out and buy it. When referring to a speaker he felt was on to something great, I'd save every penny until I could afford to buy the speaker's training tapes or attend his seminar.

One day Tom challenged my determination by offering me free materials if I would invest my last $155 dollars to attend a three-day seminar, and I did the unthinkable—I jumped at the chance. I was supported and encouraged by my parents who believed in the advantages of learning about how America's leaders achieved greatness. Even though my company didn't pick up the seminar fees, and my parents knew my sacrifice would cost practically every cent I had, they reassured me that making such a sacrifice would be incentive for me to get my money's worth.

Once again, they were right. I had invested my last dime to go to this recommended seminar, and I was determined to make the most of the speaker's teachings. Soon my sales commissions jumped from $147 per month to more than the income many of the company's other top professionals were making. Did that satisfy my hunger to learn? Absolutely not! I kept questioning highly successful people. Every time I would go to a seminar, I'd wait around after the presentation for an opportunity to personally meet and talk to the speaker. You know what I discovered? Many great people love to see the enthusiasm of newcomers. I found that those I had previously admired from afar were more than willing to talk to me about my dreams. Most importantly, I learned that great speakers take the success of their students seriously—and so do I.

I went from my whopping $147 per month selling position to top producer in my field, and then I stepped into management and ownership. When I decided to become a student of sales, and I invested in training in order to learn the proven strategies and techniques that would create success, my whole life changed. I've never been the same since.

However, management was a different story. When I got into management—everything came to a screeching halt! I thought my people would be as pumped up as I. Mistakenly, I thought my successes would mount until every manager would want to know my trade secrets. Did I have a rude awakening. Management was a whole different ballgame, and I wasn't trained in the proper methods and strategies for developing my people. The problem was, at first I didn't consider myself to be in the people-moving business at all. I was still selling a product, trying to close the sale, only my salespeople weren't buying it. They were smart enough to know a good presentation when they heard one and to recognize the fact that I was a green pea at management.

At that point, I did what many potentially great managers do early on in their new careers, I promptly lost my direction and confidence. Since that was even more uncomfortable for me than stepping out on a limb, I decided to level with my people. I was struggling! I needed time to know how to become as good a manager as I had been a salesperson, which meant discovering things about myself, first. Time for me to go on another journey—a quest to discover just what I wanted and expected from my new position as manager.

I made a list; I'm kind of a lover of lists, anyway. On my list I wrote all the things "I" wanted. My list was very "**I**" focused. It contained things like: "**I** want to make more money." **I** want more balance and control over my life!"

> It didn't take me long, though, to realize that being "**I**" focused wasn't doing much to motivate my salespeople.

It was then that I remembered the words of another of my mentors, Zig Ziglar, as he said, "You can have everything in life you want if you will just help enough other people get what they want." That was the key—what I wanted wasn't happening because the needs of my salespeople were not being met in the process.

I had always been a self-starter—a self-motivated salesperson. When suffering a sales slump, I would do whatever it took to pull myself up by my bootstraps and go back to the basics. On the other hand, if my sales were great and I was tempted to take a little break during my busy season, I'd practice self-discipline and wait for a more appropriate time. Good or bad, I was willing to do whatever it took to become successful. What puzzled me was that many of my salespeople weren't willing to do the same. Unfortunately, what many of my salespeople wanted to sit around and cry about the poor market conditions, our ineffective sales strategies or the competition's advantage. I'd often hear them say they wished they'd have another "hot" month like that one they had last year.

What were they thinking? How could anyone have a good month when all he or she thought about was the negative? I was frustrated; I had little patience and even less desire to handhold a group of men and women who weren't able or willing to motivate themselves. I felt as though I was running an adult daycare center, and I would venture to say that many of you are nodding agreement to experiencing those same feelings.

 Then I took 100 percent responsibility for improving the performance of my team.

Could it be that my salespeople wanted better but didn't know how to get it? Did they moan and complain about their lot in life because they were as lost as I was? My worries didn't stop there. Maybe I wasn't cut out to be a manager? Perhaps everybody on my sales team had simply decided they weren't going to perform at their highest level for me? What I eventually learned was that my salespeople definitely WEREN'T going to do it FOR ME! Furthermore, I didn't want them to PERFORM for me. That's for circus animals. I wanted them to be their best FOR THEMSELVES!

If I truly did want them to be successful and enjoy all life had to offer to top producing salespeople, then I had to alter my perspective—change my focus. I had to get my eyes off ME and get them on ways I could help them to become better salespeople—and in doing so create a superior sales team. I began to ask myself . . .

- What could I do to give them greater job satisfaction?
- What could I do to help them double their incomes?
- What could I do to create a better working environment?
- How could I encourage them to become more involved in life-long learning and training?

When I began thinking this way, my team's performance went through the roof. They were unbelievable! Working with them wasn't a burden any longer; it was great fun! Very rewarding. The first year, managing the health and sports facilities where I had been top salesperson—we increased our profits by 600 percent. We soon became known as one of the best companies in which to work, and recruiting the best salespeople was no problem at all.

I far exceeded the goals I wrote down on that paper my first year in sales management.

> To this day, I believe the reason I surpassed my goals was because I provided my people a way to achieve what they wanted, too.

Although my sales team was outperforming anything they had done before, I still wasn't getting what I wanted. It was a nagging discontent, but I couldn't put my finger on the cause. I kept searching.

If you're like I was when managing my people, I was so busy putting out fires that I forgot to dream. How about a little peace and quiet after a 15-hour day at the office? How about a little appreciation for organizing an effective plan that all my salespeople could easily implement? How about a good nights sleep without worrying about achieving quotas or turning in quarterly reports? At the time, I thought those sounded like pretty good dreams.

Still the nagging feeling of dissatisfaction continued. What would it take to make me happy?—Become a better manager?—Make general manager?—Take ownership? Each time one of my salespeople were recognized for outstanding performance, or when I became regional director and saw one of my managers do well because of one of the principles I taught him or her, I experienced great personal satisfaction. Suddenly, it came to me. I could achieve that kind of satisfaction every day. I finally knew what I wanted. The words of Zig Ziglar moved from my mind to my heart, and my dream became one of helping other salespeople, managers and entrepreneurs get what they wanted—achieving my dreams in the process.

Some thought I had already obtained all my wants. After all, I was a successful businessman; I lived in a great home; I had invested well; I drove a fancy car and took fun vacations. So, what was missing? The great thing about focusing on the question of what it will take to make you happy—with perseverance, you'll discovered happiness. That's just what happened.

I soon realized my desire to educate and train sales managers could be traced back to my family. Just after my 19th birthday, my father suffered a severe heart attack. Since escaping Cuba, he had single-handedly built a great business where he was the sole proprietor and only manager for his people. He had a ten-stall garage, and three gas stations that were served by his own auto-parts supply business. The problem was, with no qualified managers to care for my father's business while he was recovering, he ended up leaving the hospital to face a total collapse of his business and an overwhelming debt of over $70,000. My heart went out to my father and still breaks when I learn of other business owners and managers who have suffered similar situations. That created in me a need to be part of the solution for managers, in both large corporations and little mom and pop operations. I was then and still am a firm believer that every business needs excellent leadership.

I knew I was happiest helping others achieve, but I feared the changes I would need to take to make that happen. I wanted to be a teacher, to speak to corporations, large groups of salespeople and managers and help them to go through the changes I had already experienced. So, I sold all nine of my health and sports fitness facilities and concentrated on becoming the best sales and sales management teacher in the business. With my vocal training, I felt I would have the voice strength. With my experience, I believed I would have the background for becoming a great trainer. And, with my desire and persistence, I knew I would be able to endure the tough times. That's what got me where I am today—experiencing all the personal and professional rewards of being one of the world's top sales management trainers.

What Is Your Management Story

After hearing my story, I'd like you to think about your own personal management story. Consider these questions . . .
- What is it you want and expect from your management career?
- How do you want to be viewed by your superiors and your salespeople?
- Do you want to be seen as a manager who gets things done?
- Do you want to be viewed as a manager who is innovative and creative—progressive and proactive?
- Do you pride yourself on practicing a management style of listening and caring about the concerns of others?

If all those things describe your dreams, then what's stopping you from getting what you want?

Does fear of change hold you back from being your best?

It could be that the image you have created for yourself is in conflict with your actual management style. For example, some see themselves as being good listeners. But, ask their people what they think and you'll hear a different story. Some see themselves as perhaps being just a little bit cautious. Ask their people and they'll tell you their manager is a "dyed in the wool" traditionalist. Consider these three questions:

1. How do you perceive your management style?
2. How do your people perceive your management style?
3. Is there a huge difference between the two perceptions?

How Will This Book Help You?

Working through these chapters will help you to identify your wants and how to achieve them. You'll learn how to plan for better management and clearly communicate that plan to your people. You'll learn more about yourself and more about your people. So, if you're looking for catchy little fluff stories to repeat in your sales meetings, you may have the wrong book. If you're looking to be spoon fed with no attached responsibilities, I suspect your desire to change may not be strong enough to help you overcome the challenges. However, if you are willing to do whatever it takes to bring greater success to you and your people, you've come to the right place. This book's for you.

Taking Full Advantage of the Book

Let me share with you how to draw the greatest advantages from this book. First of all, realize that this is not a "one-sit" read through. Instead, you'll want to read, study and implement the skills presented in this book one chapter at a time. Be sure to complete the exercises at the end of each chapter. The assignments are designed to make you think, to help you discover, to assist you in your planning, to motivate you to act, and to help you evaluate what you've learned as a result of working through these management strategies. Periodically, you may want to review the strategies by re-reading a particular chapter to internalize all the information.

> Whatever you are learning, share the lessons with your team and your fellow managers. The more involved you become when reading through the book and working through the exercises, the more your enthusiasm and sales will increase; it's a highly contagious endeavor.Whatever you are learning, share the lessons with your team and your fellow managers. The more involved you become when reading through the book and working through the exercises, the more your enthusiasm and sales will increase; it's a highly contagious endeavor.

It's not necessary to look at each chapter in the order it is presented. Focus first on the areas where you need the most improvement. It is assumed in these chapters that you are ready and willing to make some changes for the betterment of your sales team. You may find that some of those changes will be strictly within your professional management career and some may spill over into your personal life.

These are some steps to immediately consider in this first chapter. Ask yourself the following questions:

1. What is it that you really want from your management career?
2. How will getting what you want affect your career and the careers of your salespeople?
3. How will greater achievement affect your family life or personal lifestyle?
4. What are the goals you'll need to achieve in order to get what you want?
5. What are the daily steps you'll need to take in order to achieve those goals?
6. How will you measure your success?
7. If necessary, how will you monitor and adjust your plan?
8. Who will you solicit to help you develop your plan of action?
9. What are the consequences and rewards for following your plan?
10. Do you have a vivid picture of what success will be like for you?

Visualize Becoming A Successful Manager

It's important at this stage of the game that you are able to visualize your success. I learned this a long time ago from a close mentor and friend. He taught me to capture all the passion I had for sales by vividly picturing my success. The picture kept me emotionally involved with my dream, and my emotions fueled my passion to keep working toward my sales goals. I constantly reminded myself of the words of author Cherie Carter-Scott: "Extraordinary people visualize not what is possible or probable, but rather what is impossible. And by visualizing the impossible, they begin to see it as possible."

Every night before I went to bed I'd close my eyes and allow myself some important daydreaming time. I would envision this huge picture in my head. In as much detail and color as I could picture, I would see myself how I wanted to become, not how I was at the time—a salesperson making $147 a month. That wasn't going to get me to my dream. That's one of the key things I did—in my mind pictures, I saw myself as I was CAPABLE of becoming, not who I was at the time. One of the greatest thinkers of all times, Goethe, says, "Look at a man the way that he is, he only becomes worse. But look at him as if he were what he could be, and then he becomes what he should be."

Soon, I was able to do for myself what my parents had always done for me as a child. They saw my future potential as if it was something I had already achieved. They could see the picture of what I COULD become instead of making judgments based on what I was. They didn't see a young boy who couldn't speak English, who had difficulties communicating with peers, someone with a poor self-image who didn't have the nicest clothes or fanciest car. No, instead they saw an intelligent, honest, courageous young man who lived in America where anything was possible—even for an immigrant. They saw determination within my anger and frustration. They saw a compassionate heart within my shyness. Knowing how my parents and peers believed in me, I was able to create those pictures of myself that helped me to be the best manager and leader for my people. Now, when I lose my momentum, I just allow myself to dream. More than anything else, that gets me fired up about what I want.

I believe in you the way my parents believed in me. My goal for you is that you too recognize that each and every one of you has greatness within. Throughout this book, you'll be reviewing some things you may have known for a long time—but that's what the great ones do—they review things. It never hurts to be reminded of things that have worked for you in the past and are currently working for other managers. As you read, you'll be internalizing new ideas about how to better lead your people. Realize that there will be some information that may not apply to you; there will be some information that you will feel doesn't fit your management methods or company culture. That's okay.

Think of this book as a menu of "little gems" for you and your people. Take what gems are precious to you and your team and leave the rest for another time. Don't hesitate to share ideas with your peers. Even if you don't think they fit your particular management style, your associates may feel just the opposite.

> My hope for you as you begin the journey through these pages is that you discover the power of change, the value of open-mindedness and an overwhelming passion for leading your people. There are no random principles and strategies contained within these pages, but, rather, ones that are intended to transform you from manager to leader—leading your people to out-think, out-perform, out-manage and out-produce the competition.

So, let's begin our journey together.

Working Through the Process--Chapter One

❖ List five of the most important things you want from your management career.

1. _____

2. _____

3. _____

4. _____

5. _____

❖ How do you expect this book will help you achieve the above wants?

1. _____

2. _____

3. _____

4. _____

5. _____

❖ How do your superiors perceive your management style? How do your subordinates perceive your management style? Is there a disparity between the two? Why?

Superiors Perceptions

_____

_____

Subordinates Perceptions

_____

_____

What is the disparity? Why?

_____

_____

❖ How would you like to be perceived by your superiors? Subordinates?

Superiors

_____

_____

Subordinates

_____

_____

❖ What changes do you need to make in order to align those perceptions?

_____

_____

❖ What are the strengths and weaknesses of your sales team?

Strengths	Weaknesses
_____	_____
_____	_____
_____	_____
_____	_____

❖ How does your management style and methods contribute to the strengths and weaknesses of your salespeople?

Strengths:

_____

_____

Weaknesses:

_____

_____

❖ After having read and studied this book, I expect...

_____

_____

❖ In order to meet and exceed my expectations, I will commit to...

_____

_____

CHAPTER TWO

Are You Maintaining An Average Team or Creating an Exceptional One?

"Tell somebody something; they'll forget. Show them, and they might remember.   But, INVOLVE them, and they'll understand!"

Old Chinese Proverb

Chapter Highlights:

▶ Getting Support and Total Involvement from Your Salespeople
▶ The Six Top-Ranked Problems of Today's Sales Teams
▶ Overcoming the Problems and Leading Your Team
▶ Taking the Test to Get the Lesson
▶ Do's and Don'ts of Leadership

Much of the success of today's large corporations and even small businesses is dependent upon its salespeople. Each salesperson's ability to succeed is inhibited or enhanced by the efforts of his or her co-workers. The enthusiastic productivity of the team—or the lack of it— influences each salesperson's attitude and motivation. Whether positive or negative, that attitude and motivation is highly contagious. It's an awesome challenge and responsibility that sales managers face—developing their salespeople into an efficient, superior team of professionals. However, with the proper training and knowledge, having a team of top producers is not a pipe dream!

Your sales team can be as dynamic or dependent as you decide— based on your ability to lead.

Applying the Old Chinese Proverb quoted at the beginning of this chapter will lead to sound leadership principles.

 Get yourself and your salespeople involved, and you'll be well on your way to creating and managing an effective—no an OUTSTANDING—sales team.

Unfortunately, it's easier said than done! How do you get your salespeople enthusiastically involved in prospecting when they think they just don't have the knack for it? How do you get your salespeople to practice consistent follow-up when business is great and they feel no sense of urgency? Or, how do you convince your salespeople to establish good follow-up practices when they already have more customers than they can effectively serve? If you've been managing a team of salespeople for any length of time, I'm sure you have made the following discovery: It's virtually impossible for you to single-handedly offer all the encouragement, mentoring, coaching and support every salesperson on your team requires. There just aren't enough hours in a day.

Leadership is not an individual endeavor, though. You'll need help from the experts and support from everybody on your team in order to be an outstanding manager.

The following will help you as you change from simply "managing" your team to actually "leading" them:
1. Each member can contribute.
2. Take team objectives seriously and hold yourself accountable.
3. Support one another.
4. Break down long-term aims into short-term projects.
5. Assign and clearly communicate project deadlines.
6. Decide on and hire only those people capable of significantly contributing to the team.
7. Provide bonding opportunities for members of your sales team and yourself. Social gatherings are great—perhaps sporting events or a company softball team. Create opportunities for you and your salespeople to get to know one another outside the working environment.
8. Find an advisor or mentor outside the team to act as a consultant.
9. Fix goals that are measurable.
10. Always reward team members on merit—not on reputation.

Are you ready to become an exceptional leader? Are you willing to do what it takes to develop an exceptional sales team? If so, I'm ready to be your private coach to successful management. Let's begin!

Investigative Selling

If you've read or listened to any of my other material, you'll recognize that I'm a great believer in the investigative approach to sales, as taught in my first book *Investigative Selling*. This book is no different. In this chapter I've investigated the challenges faced by today's corporate teams. According to a recent Towers Perrin Sales Effectiveness Study, there are six major challenges today's teams need to overcome. Ranked in order are the top six challenges of corporate teams:

#1 Ranked Problem: Overlap/confusion in responsibilities and territory definition
#2 Ranked Problem: Unequal distribution of work/performance, but equal distribution of rewards
#3 Ranked Problem: Diminished accountability and/or motivation
#4 Ranked Problem: Poor information sharing
#5 Ranked Problem: Unclear compensation structure
#6 Ranked Problem: Time spent on team building at the expense of customer relationship building

We've identified six of the top-ranked problems that corporate leaders reported having in the development and growth of their sales teams. Now what? Now that you've identified the concerns of your salespeople as they work together on your team, what are your options? What is your plan of action? They are looking toward your leadership to help them work through these problems and become a unified, efficient team. Let's go back to the problems and focus on some solutions.

Overcoming the Six Top-Ranked Problems of Today's Corporate Teams

What can you do to overcome the #1 Ranked Problem of overlap and confusion in responsibility and territory definition?

• <u>Define individual territories and responsibilities up front</u>. For example, let's say one salesperson has been working with a branch office manager. When it comes time to make the buying decision, the branch manager refers the salesperson to his or her superior who is located at headquarters. The problem is that headquarters lies within the territory of a co-worker who has been working with the vice president of sales. You need to have a plan that helps your people deal effectively and fairly with these types of overlaps.

> Your salespeople need to know what is considered acceptable and fair. For greater ownership, allow the team to develop their own boundaries and ground rules.

If you're in retail and a salesperson's territory is a particular area of the sales floor, or his or her territory consists of certain items such as electronics or appliances, this can still be a challenge. The salesperson needs to know how to handle a customer who moves from his or her territory into that of another salesperson. For instance, what is team policy if the customer changes from wanting to purchase a television, to looking at a computer and their change of mind moves them out of that particular salesperson's floor territory? Make sure that you address those situations with your team so they can decide and agree upon what is fair and acceptable to all parties.

• <u>Role-play possible scenarios and discover sound problem-solving techniques ahead of time so that all members are aware of what to do if territorial overlap occurs</u>. You can't possibly know ahead of time the various situations that will occur over territory disputes. You can anticipate them based on your experiences working on teams yourself and previous challenges encountered by team members you've managed in the past.   But, no matter how much you anticipate recurring situations, about the time you believe you have identified any possible situation a new one will crop up. To prepare you and your team for problems in overlapping territory disputes, consider the following:
1. Communicate your past experiences, team efforts to overcome the challenges, and the results of those efforts.
2. Role-play what you would do in similar situations.
3. Set the stage for new solutions to new challenges.

- Establish a method of arbitration to fairly intervene should the issues become clouded. One of the keys to effective leadership is to teach your sales team to fairly resolve problems. Encourage them to intervene quickly when questions arise. Take care of the problems before they become stumbling blocks to the entire team's productivity. Encourage them to establish their own arbitration board of peers to resolve team problems. In doing so, they will have much more ownership in the team's efforts and feel individually responsible for their own successes and setbacks.

- Allow your sales team to plan and implement their own success, then support their plan. Give them ownership and commitment to the entire team. This goes back to that old Chinese Proverb again that speaks to the need to keep others INVOLVED.

> The most difficult thing for you as a sales manager might be to support your salespeople's plan.

Why? Well, what if you will need to defend their plan to your superiors, and there are many at the top who oppose your methods of leadership? Will you be willing to stand up for your team? Or, what if their plan doesn't achieve the expected positive results, will you be able to step out of the way and let your team work it through? That's trust— that's support to the highest degree. It's difficult for sales managers to set aside their own strategies when they are outvoted by their sales team, especially if the team has had a few setbacks along the way that may have put that manager in an awkward position.

Let me leave you with a last note regarding the #1 ranked problem of territory definition and overlap. Do the work up front. Anticipate challenges before they occur, and prepare your team to effectively handle similar situations.

Okay, moving to the #2 Ranked Problem of unequal distribution of work/performance but equal distribution of rewards. What can you as a great leader do to help your sales team work through this one?

- Realize if the work is in proportion to the rewards, it doesn't matter if the work is unequal. The question to ask yourself then is "Do the rewards reflect each member's efforts?"

- <u>Sometimes, the most unequal thing to do is to treat everybody equally</u>. While you are looking at the bigger picture of the team's quotas, the team's production, the team's successes and setbacks, don't forget to reward the individual's effort or encourage and support the individual salesperson who is struggling. If one salesperson's efforts are far and above what was required, publicly recognize his or her efforts.

> Appreciate outstanding performance both privately and publicly.

In other words, be attentive to the needs of the individual as well as the team.

- <u>One member's expertise may require only a 10 percent contribution. Another's may necessitate a 90 percent contribution</u>. Each salesperson has fulfilled his or her part if that salesperson has completed his or her own total contribution—no matter the percentage. Recognize that salesperson for making the full commitment, but reward individually based on the percentage of effort required of that particular salesperson. Make sure the rewards equal the contributions, and forget the notion that all will receive the identical and equal amount.

As a leader, what can you do about the #3 Ranked Problem of diminished accountability and motivation of the team?

- <u>The more your sales team achieves, the more motivated they will be to continue at their peak performance</u>. That's the great thing about success, it simply encourages greater and greater levels of success. The difficulties arise when you step into a situation where there hasn't been much success and you are left the dismal, tiring job of motivating salespeople whose morale is low and interest even lower. That's where this book will help you. Let's face it, it's easy to lead people who continually and consistently achieve success. As you study this information (notice I said STUDY), your knowledge and leadership skills will get better and better. Share your newly acquired knowledge, and it won't be long before you'll notice your salespeople's performance will improving proportionately to your own as a leader.

- <u>Increase accountability by basing your performance measurement on specific activities and behaviors—not just on your salespeople's end results</u>. Although you need to stay focused on your destination, it's the journey that counts. If salespeople are so focused on their monthly quota that they loose sight of the daily activities required to get them there, then the end result won't be the one you desire. Encourage your team to look at every new day as a fresh start. In doing so, they won't rest on their laurels after a very successful sale to one of their tough accounts. They also won't turn a one-time disappointment into a three-week depression. Defining your team's success on a daily basis allows everybody to come to work in the morning with renewed enthusiasm and commitment.

- <u>Establish what individual activities it will take to accomplish the goals of the entire sales team</u>. Involve the entire team in goal sitting and achieving positive end results. This reminds me of a story I once read about the Seattle Special Olympics where nine contestants, all physically or mentally challenged, were assembled at the starting line for the 100-yard dash. As they began their race, one young lad stumbled and fell, rolling several times on the hard asphalt. When the other competitors heard his cries, they all turned around and went back to help him complete his goal by linking arms and walking together to the finish line. Every person in the stadium gave them a 10-minute standing ovation. That's what I'd call an outstanding effort that involved the entire team.

- <u>Use the tools of measurement that are available in your organization to track sales performance</u>. Some of the tools I've used in the past have been an Activity Tracking Form; a Win/Loss Review Form; or a Self-Evaluation Sheet (sample forms provided at end of chapter).

> Make sure that whatever you use to measure success, your expectations are clearly communicated and regularly reviewed. Don't allow a minor slip to continue until it becomes a major setback. I always say, **"Salespeople respect what managers inspect!"**

- <u>Avoid negative judgment</u>.

> Instead, lead by example and encourage individual problem solving.

Be open in your discussions about times when you may have experienced similar setbacks, and share with your team what you did to conquer them. When encouraging them to honestly evaluate themselves, don't stand in judgment of their weaknesses. Congratulate their successes, and find ways to help them fairly look at their areas of improvement. The effectiveness of a true leader is seen in the expressions and attitudes of those on his or her team.

> Make the following a habit: whenever a member of your team leaves your presence, he or she leaves feeling good about him/herself, hopeful of future performance, and eager to innovate new ideas, behaviors and activities to bring about greater levels of success.

Moving on now, let's look at the #4 Ranked Problem of poor information sharing. Although it's easy to make sure you communicate the necessary information, what is easy to do is also easy not to do.

- <u>Be sure you have clearly established company goals and objectives, and then bring those goals and objectives in alignment with your sales team</u>. For example, let's say your company is currently emphasizing customer service. Your sales team has set a sizeable quota for the month. Because of this quota, they may be tempted to take shortcuts and not provide the proper customer service. What happens? The goals of your team will be in direct conflict with those of your company. It's the job of the sales manager to emphasize and reward outstanding customer service in order to reinforce the achievement of the company goals—even in the face of equally important team objectives.

- <u>Encourage collaboration and cooperation both within and outside your sales team</u>.

I believe one of the most powerful management tools to have as a leader is the ability to be flexible, accepting of others differences and appreciative of opposing opinions.

When you are that kind of leader, those on your sales team will extend the same courtesy to their co-workers and pull together as a true team.

- <u>Value each salesperson's innovation and recognize every idea as a possibility</u>. This creates a comfortable and safe team environment.

When creative thinkers are given no outlet for their unique insights, they often move on to work for the competition.

Perhaps they feel that with their competition they will be given license to achieve, to oppose without judgment, to create vision for their team.

- <u>Teams cease to be teams if only the top performers are rewarded for their achievements</u>. Spread the wealth! Find ways to celebrate the individual successes of the newcomers to the team.

Often times, a newcomer's enthusiasm and high energy can be a boost to the increased performance of everybody. Reward them for that.

On the other hand, don't always expect top producers to contribute more than their fair share with no rewards or special incentives.

Moving on to the #5 Ranked Problem many sales teams have—unclear compensation structures. This one can be tough, but your salespeople will work with you if you've already demonstrated your willingness to be a supportive leader.

- <u>Encourage your salespeople to be customer minded</u>. As their leader— the most effective way to emphasize customer service is to lead the way—teach by example. Think of your salespeople as your customers, and serve them well. Be . . .

1. Respectful
2. Attentive
3. Responsive to their needs
4. Appreciative
5. Willing to share in their losses as well as their wins

- <u>Nobody said compensation always had to be in dollars</u>. Most top salespeople leave an organization because they didn't feel appreciated and valued. Contrary to what we've been told, it usually isn't because that top producer was lacking in commissions or base pay.

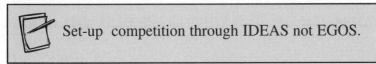 When was the last time you praised your salespeople?

Do you make it a point to thank them for doing a great job for the company and making you look good? Even if it is his or her job, everybody likes to be singled out and given recognition and praise now and then.

- <u>Get to know your salespeople, and discover what motivates them</u>. Structure compensation to fit the specific needs of your salespeople. As a leader, that's being customer focused. You are now focusing on the individual needs of your people to improve the collective needs of your team.

- <u>Discuss and make public the rewards of those at the top</u>. At the same time, make sure you set the stage for healthy competition.

Set-up competition through IDEAS not EGOS.

Finally, let's look at the #6 Ranked Problem salespeople across the country stated they had when working in teams. The time spent on team building often came at the expense of customer relationship building. This problem is greatly increased or decreased depending upon your leadership skills.

- <u>If you choose those on your sales team wisely, your company's customers will be richly rewarded</u>. I'm going to discuss ways to recruit in Chapter Three, but it's your customers (the salespeople) or lack of them that will reflect your ability to make quality choices in recruiting new salespeople.

> I hope we are way past the days of filling chairs—or the thinking that any warm body will do.

I do realize that when you are recruiting salespeople, it may be impossible to get a team of top producers. It may not even be desirable to do so.

> For most managers, your challenge will be to DEVELOP top producers—not just RECRUIT them.

- <u>Recognize that you can't do it all</u>. In Chapter 3, I'll show you how to find the experts to help you develop your people. That gives you enough free time to focus on the internal needs of your sales team.

- <u>If you provide exceptional administrative and financial support for your sales team; if your number one goal is to keep an open, trusting relationship—your salespeople will learn by your example</u>. Their positive morale will be reflected in the relationships they create and maintain with their customers as well.

Today's sales managers, today's leaders, aren't about trying to "control" their people. What **great** leaders do is LEAD and then get out of the way of their people. They facilitate; they inspire; they actively support their salespeople through the challenges and changes they'll need to overcome in today's marketplace.

Does this method seem much different from the management style you are currently practicing? If so, you have some work ahead of you. Be patient with yourself. Give yourself time to make it through that learning curve. Expect to revert to old, ineffective management patterns when you're under extreme stress—in a crisis you might become that "controller" again. That's okay! If your salespeople know you are a work in progress, they'll be patient with you. It's easy to forgive others' mistakes when they have first forgiven yours. What I mean is, if you are patient with your salespeople when they have setbacks and are experiencing difficulties in their performance, they'll be more understanding of the personal challenges some of you may face when attempting to change your management style.

The most difficult step is recognizing you have work to do and being willing to take the test to get the lesson.

> It would be interesting to know if the way you perceive yourself as a manager is how your salespeople perceive you, wouldn't it?

Some of you may not think you have a managing or leadership style, but you do. You all do. Some of you may think your management methods may be positive, and you don't understand why you keep getting negative results. Well, perhaps you are inadvertently doing things that you believe to be POSITIVELY motivating, but because you haven't gotten to know your salespeople, you don't know what moves them to action.

Keep in mind that you are, as I said before, a work in progress. At the risk of repetition, I'll once again quote the words of my mentor and friend, Zig Ziglar: "You need a checkup from the neck up." Ask yourself these questions:

1. Do you take the time to clearly communicate your expectations to your sales team and each individual member?
2. Are you able to adjust your management style to the individual needs of your sales team?
3. Will you back up your sales team if it means going against the "sacred cows," or the more traditional thinkers of the company?
4. Are you a paper pusher or a people developer? Which is your management style?
5. Can you delegate and then get out of the way of your salespeople?
6. Have you set up measurable goals and realistic expectations?
7. Do you give positive strokes to create positive folks?
8. Do you treat your salespeople with respect?
9. Have you created an environment that is both positive and productive?
10. Are you ready to do what it takes to step from management into leadership? What makes leaders different? General Norman Schwarzkopf says, "A great leader is an average individual who is extremely well prepared when an incredible event occurs."

What is the difference between a manager and a leader?

An effective **manager** understands the desired result and coordinates the tasks and activities it will take to accomplish that goal. A great **leader** inspires others to want to accomplish the desired goal and provides the means by which it can be done.

Become a true leader. Move from management to leadership. Commit yourself to lifelong learning. How?

Become a student, majoring in professional leadership and personal development.

Do you remember when educators used to say that you had to know your 3 Rs (**r**eading, **r**iting, and **r**ithmetic)?   Well, I have developed the 3 **R**s to effective leadership:

RECOGNIZE the need for primary and ongoing training for you and your salespeople. Implement new and innovative skills and strategies.

READ and study peak-performers in your industry. Organize a library for your salespeople. Let them share in all the benefits of becoming students as well.

REMEMBER to celebrate the successes of your salespeople—both publicly and privately. Let them know how much you value their contributions to the team and to the customers!

Let me share with you some tips in team development. Just a few **DO'S** and **DON'TS**.

DO—change your leadership style according to the needs of your sales team. If your team needs more of a hands-on style of coaching, stay a little closer to the team's decision-making and implementation. If your team prefers to problem-solve and learn through experience, step back and let them learn through trial and error. Be the coach your salespeople indicate fits their needs the best.

DON'T—look to blame others for team setbacks, but look first to see what part your style of leadership played in their setback. If you are eager to share in their wins—be willing to accept and defend their losses.

DO—emphasize and support team values.
DON'T—skirt issues to ignore or avoid conflict.
DO—respond positively to novel and creative ideas.
DON'T—kill the spirit of "maverick" thinkers.
DO—encourage individual and group learning.
DON'T—miss opportunities to lead by example.

Do all these things and you'll be the type of leader known for instilling team spirit. As you're working on your skills of managing an outstanding team of professionals, know you have now joined the ranks of outstanding leaders. Who knows, before long people could be studying **your** management methods and strategies.

Working Through the Process--Chapter Two

❖ The Top Six Challenges Faced by Today's Corporate Teams

1. _____ and/or Confusion in Responsibilities and _____ Definition
2. _____ Distribution of Work and/or Performance but _____ Distribution of Rewards
3. Diminished _____ and/or _____
4. Poor _____ Sharing
5. Unclear _____ Structure
6. Time Spent on ____ _____ at the Expense of _____ _____ Building

❖ How are you currently addressing the six ranked top challenges by today's sales teams?

#1 Ranked Challenge:

_____

_____

#2 Ranked Challenge:

_____

_____

#3 Ranked Challenge:

_____

_____

#4 Ranked Challenge:

_____

_____

#5 Ranked Challenge:

_____

_____

#6 Ranked Challenge:

_____

_____

❖ List at least five changes you could make in your management style and methods to increase productivity and profits.

1. _____

2. _____

3. _____

4. _____

5. _____

❖ How are you practicing the "3 Rs" of management?

First "R" = Recognize the need for professional and ongoing training for you and your salespeople. Implement new and innovative skills and strategies.

This Year's Training Schedule:

_____

_____

Second "R" = Read and study peak performers in your industry. Organize a library for your salespeople. Let them share in all the benefits of becoming students as well.

Who are your mentors? How are you implementing their management methods?

_____

_____

Third "R" = Remember to celebrate the successes of your salespeople -- both publicly and privately. Let them know how much you value their contributions to the team and to the customers.

How will you celebrate you and your team's successes? Monthly? Quarterly? Annually?

_____

_____

❖ The Questions Outstanding Managers Ask Themselves

❑ Do I take the time to clearly _____ my _____ of the sales team and each individual member?
❑ Am I able to _____ my _____ _____ to the individual needs of my _____ ____?
❑ Will I ____ __ my sales team if it means going against the _____ ____ of the company?
❑ Am I a _____ _____ or a _____ _____?
❑ Can I _____ and then get out of the way of my salespeople?
❑ Have I set up _____ goals and _____ expectations?
❑ Do I give positive _____ to create positive _____?
❑ Do I treat my _____ with _____?
❑ Have I created an _____ that is both _____ and _____?
❑ Am I ready to do what it takes to step from _____ to _____?

CHAPTER THREE

Recruit the Best--Develop the Rest

"What I do best is share my enthusiasm."
                          Bill Gates

Chapter Highlights:

▶ Defining the Well-matched Candidate
▶ "Eight Point Lookout" for New Recruits
▶ E.S.P. Signals the Point to Winning Potential
▶ Writing Effective Recruitment Ads
▶ Designing A Recruitment Plan
▶ Sample Rejection Letter
▶ Recipe for Success

Before you begin recruiting, run through your attitude pre-check list.

✔ If you were the candidate looking for a new sales position, would **you** want to work for you?
✔ If you were a new recruit, would you consider it a privilege to be a part of your current sales team?
✔ If not—why not? Change places with your recruits and look at yourself through their eyes; it's a good way to prepare yourself for the recruiting process.

Keep in mind, while you are looking for sharp salespeople—they are looking for a progressive, innovative leader as well.

> That GREAT recruit is making judgments about your management style while you're evaluating his or her skills. They are checking out your philosophies, requirements and the working environment you provide.

Sharp salespeople are the ones who are sizing you up at the same time you are sizing them up. So, be ready to exceed their expectations. Within this chapter, you'll learn how to create eagerness on the part of your new salespeople. We'll review where you go and what you do to recruit potentially great people. I'll be asking you to examine and identify what type of salespeople would be perfect candidates for your existing team.

In the early recruiting stages, it's important to determine exactly what is needed to complete and complement your team. It's helpful to write out an accurate job description so you can identify and attract the types of salespeople you want. The mind is trained to serve your wants and needs, so focus on whom you want and your mind will create opportunities for you to attract that type of person. Unfortunately, many managers give far too much thought to the type of salespeople they don't want, and those are the ones they end up attracting.

> Set your sites on your ideal candidate. Define his or her characteristics and attributes. Visualize what that salesperson would look like and how they would produce.

Target and focus the recruiting process on who you want, and you'll recognize those candidates when you meet them.

If you are fortunate to have within your organization a human resources department, solicit its help in the recruiting process. Your human resources expert can let you know if anyone inside your organization has expressed an interest in moving into sales. A good human resources manager makes it his or her job to constantly network within the company.

As you look through applications, keep in mind that the perfect match on paper won't be the end all to your recruiting problems. What's on paper may sound great, but there may be shortcomings once you get face-to-face with the candidate. Doubts can be created by something as simple as a hunch or that little voice that says, "You better rethink this one." It has been my experience that listening to that little warning voice usually saves a lot of turmoil down the road.

> Great managers have great instincts. More importantly, they follow those instincts during the recruiting process.

If the resume looks good, but that voice is whispering, "Hmmm, something about this candidate's personality or background needs to be looked at closer," listen to that inner voice and take a closer look. It could mean looking for a more suitable recruit elsewhere. To put it simply—trust your instincts. That is the makings of an outstanding leader.

You might be asking yourself, "How will I know when I have the perfect match?" You won't! You can anticipate what your salespeople need in a new team member. You can identify what type of person will make the best fit with your company. But, no matter how hard you try to find the profile that creates a perfect match, your relationship is on a trial basis. Like any relationship, it takes time to determine whether you and your new recruit have made the right decision. Give the recruit and yourself that time.

Frequently, those you doubt will be successful on your sales team and will hit the ground running. They'll be able to get along fine with other salespeople and turn out to be great team players. On the other hand, those you see as future top performers often let you down. There is just no way to tell. If you are looking for that perfect salesperson, you may have a long wait.

> Why not plan to recruit good people who are open to learning and flexible to change, then, through expert training and ongoing coaching, develop them into great salespeople?

Here's a little secret, sometimes the so-called "perfect" employee isn't what you're looking for, anyway. How many companies have benefited from an employee's mistake? How many inventions and creations do we enjoy as a result of someone's goof-up? Unfortunately, we are so busy looking for perfection that often times the hidden value in the mistake escapes us. That's exactly what happened to Dr. John Pemberton. Dr. Pemberton lived in the late 1800s, and, if the truth were known, had no formal education as a doctor but knew more about herbs and medicines during those times than most formally educated doctors. He experimented with extracts, fruits, nuts and leaves and created better tasting medicines that cured a myriad of ailments. In the process of formulating a new pain reliever, Dr. Pemberton concocted a syrup made with a dash of cocaine along with his usual fruits and nuts. All customers had to do was mix it with water. Unfortunately, the syrup wasn't selling and Dr. Pemberton was about to give up on the idea. About that time, a new clerk accidentally mixed the syrup with carbonated water and served it to a client. That billion-dollar mistake is now being offered in almost every restaurant, grocery store and vending machine around the world. You'd recognize the syrup today as Coca-Cola.

> Although you do want to make good choices for your sales team, don't discount those who think a bit differently or seem more radical than the rest on your team. They may bring you a whole different perspective.

It's okay to veer from the norm, but have a criteria to go by when recruiting. The following are some things to examine when defining that well-matched candidate for your organization:

1. Decide how much formal education, if any, will be necessary.

    In some positions, a candidate's experience will be much more important than his or her formal education. In others, you might need recruits to be certified or licensed, requiring a more formal background. Make sure you verify the recruit's resume information. The more carefully you check references and verify past histories in education and experience, the less likely it is you'll be disappointed by someone who believes in stretching a two-credit, college course into a four-year degree. Today's sales world is quite competitive. Many salespeople are feeling the pressures of higher standards and the demands of companies requiring greater experience levels. Unfortunately, this can create a situation where candidates feel forced to exaggerate their qualifications.

2. Decide what special training would benefit the company.

    If you have previously recruited from top-notch schools, give them an opportunity to repeat the experience by providing another new candidate. It never hurts to develop strong relationships with placement people and use them regularly as a recruiting base. Soon, they'll get to know your wants and needs and begin selecting the cream of the crop especially for you, allowing you to jump ahead of your competitors. Be sure you look at the section of an application or resume that addresses special training. It's that training that may differentiate the best from the average.

3. <u>Determine how much experience is necessary for success in this position</u>.

It is not only how much experience recruits have but under what conditions they gained the experience. For example, you may find a recruit with impressive credentials who single-handedly achieved great strides with his or her previous company; however, the recruit was not a team player and his or her knowledge only served to create hard feelings in other salespeople. Or, you might be looking for a strong individual who is a self-starter, and this recruit works better under close supervision.

4. <u>Know what kind of knowledge base would be ideal</u>.

I'm not just talking about industry knowledge, either. It could be knowledge of . . .
- Area
- Products and Services
- Marketplace
- General Sales
- Life Experience, etc. . .

5. <u>Set in your mind how you want that candidate to function within your team</u>.
What should be his or her strengths?

Should he or she be a self-starter?

Does the position you are trying to fill require someone to come in and simply take over? If so, you may not have the time or desire to handhold a salesperson incapable of taking immediate action. If you have a great recruit with good potential, you may want to place him or her with a more seasoned mentor and temporarily restructure the duties.

Will they need to take instruction well?

I remember a time in sales, and it wasn't that long ago, when the instruction most new salespeople received was here's some information about the product— here's your territory—go get 'em! It was up to the salesperson to ask questions and observe the culture within that organization. Thank goodness, many of today's organizations provide both in-house coaching and outside training for their new recruits. Discover how well this person is able to follow instructions and how willing he or she is to make adjustments and changes. That will determine how efficiently the recruit will adapt to the ways and adjust to the culture of your company.

What about their ability to be a creative problem-solver?

When given a problem, many recruits are able to find solutions. How are they at finding the problems, though? How innovative are they? Does this recruit seem the type who would stick to more traditional solutions when your team is based on more progressive thinking? If so, don't be too quick to discount his or her value. If the recruit is strong enough to stand up for the opposing viewpoint, he or she just might go against the norm and be the one to give your sales team the bigger picture by playing the "devil's advocate."

How about their communication skills?

It is absolutely essential that your people have strong communication skills. You'll get a good idea of how they speak in the interview, but it is often hard to evaluate a person's ability to write, listen and observe during the recruiting process. Those skills are often more important than their ability to speak.

Are they organized? Is that important to you?

Disorganization in a company can be costing you a lot of money. Many salespeople suffer the challenges of being unorganized. If you were quick to forgive disorganization, you may have to be the same when it comes to the myriad of missed opportunities that disorganization causes. How many accounts are lost due to disorganized salespeople who fail to serve them properly? How much time do you spend hounding your salespeople to turn in their reports or paperwork on time and in good order?

Are you looking for a risk-taker?

Just one risk-taker can greatly influence the productivity of the entire team. Others on your sales force who may hesitate to take a chance will see the positive results your risk-taker is getting because he or she was willing to step out. Perhaps the risk taker landed the account that everybody else thought was impossible. Or, maybe he or she came up with a new idea that worked wonders when demonstrating that hard-to-sell item in your product line. Risk-takers can be the catalyst for great innovation.

Do you need someone who can work alone?

Or, will you feel more comfortable with a closer style of management?

6. <u>What technological base will they need to have</u>?
Is your business so computer oriented that if one were computer challenged he or she would be unable to function on your sales team? Or, is there a certain software program recruits will need special training with in order to complete required reports? If so, you'll need to know their skills and they'll need to know your programs.

7. <u>How much money will this position pay</u>?
Make sure you give yourself room to promote the new recruit or offer monetary incentives in the position. Sometimes the best and fastest way to build a superior sales force is to—well frankly—steal them, and in that case you may be facing a higher beginning salary or commission. Be flexible. If you recruit someone who will generate a lot more business because of his or her extensive experience or additional training, pay proportionately.

8. <u>Speaking of advancement—what is the recruit's opportunity for advancement in this position</u>?
There is nothing worse than feeling trapped in a position with nowhere to go but out the door. When this happens, that is usually

where the ambitious and innovative end up going—and you've lost a good recruit because you didn't have a clear pathway for advancement.

9. What related skills will be required?

Is it important in this position that they know how to write well, have strong verbal skills and active listening skills? Will you need someone who is an excellent telemarketing person? Perhaps you're looking for someone who is analytical and logic based. Or, is it office skills or someone good at math that would best fill the position? Establish your needs before you begin the recruiting process.

10. What and who will be the reporting structure?

If they will be directly reporting to another, make sure that person participates in the recruiting process as well. YOU could get along with certain types of salespeople, but that might not be what their direct supervisor wants. Before recruiting takes place, develop your candidate profile together so that whomever recruits report to, that person won't be disappointed with your selection.

11. What are the salaries of the top performers in your company?

You can use this in the recruiting process, but only if you feel it reasonable that those same figures could soon be earned by your new recruit. If not, you are being dishonest with the new recruit when you boast such figures. In the future, their disappointment and discouragement will begin to show in their sales results.

Following these guidelines before you begin the recruiting process can mean an extended recruitment time.

But, outstanding leaders know that taking the time to qualify their recruits up front will mean they won't have to suffer the consequences later.

Do your homework, and do it well in advance of any recruiting. The information you gather will lead you to great recruiting practices.

Once you've done your homework, where do you find great recruits? Let me give you my system. I call it my "EIGHT POINT LOOKOUT" for new recruits.

1. **LOOKOUT** for recruits within the company.
    There are plenty of non-salespeople types within your organization
    who sell everyday. For example, customer service people sell your
    salespeople, products and company to those who need answers or
    concerns addressed. Maintenance people or order-entry clerks are also
    an excellent recruiting source. They are looking to move up, so many
    will be more willing to adapt to the culture of your established team.

2. **LOOKOUT** for recruiting possibilities with your professional
    connections.
    Who are the other people you meet in the course of doing business?
    Perhaps they are your vendors, your past and current clients—even
    those prospects who believe in your products and/or services. What
    about those with whom you network at chamber meetings? They are a
    rich pool of recruiting possibilities.

3. **LOOKOUT** for great referrals.
    Ask members of your sales team to recommend candidates for the
    position. It's a great way to let them personally pick their own co-
    workers. Sell them on building a high-quality sales team.

4. **LOOKOUT** for salespeople who may want to return to your company
    under your leadership.
    Former sales representatives have the advantage of inside knowledge,
    which can substantially cut down on your training efforts.

5. **LOOKOUT** for recruits in free employment services.
    They can screen candidates for you. Most of the employment
    companies are regularly exposed to young hopefuls who would make
    great candidates for your sales team.

6. **LOOKOUT** for recruits in creative advertising opportunities.
    Here's an idea—when you are reading through your company's trade
    journals, take a look at who is looking for a change. Many of them
    advertise in the classifieds of those journals.

7. **LOOKOUT** for headhunters, they'll be looking out for you.
    Mostly, these types of services are reserved for upper management. Be

careful when using their services; some can charge outlandish fees when you could have recruited that same level worker through less expensive means.

8. **LOOKOUT** for customer and personal recruiting recommendations. I've found that your good customers can recommend some great people, or they could even be interested themselves.

 Ask a casual question to your customer, like "Who do you know who would be interested in a great sales opportunity with our company?"

Knowing where to go is only half the battle, the other half is how to recognize the excellent recruits when they come knocking at your door? I use my **E.S.P.** The following are **E.S.P.** signals that point to winning potential in the raw recruit—by raw, I'm not referring to a physical condition. How can you identify winning potential in the salesperson with no experience? Through **E.S.P.**

1. **E**agerness—I believe this is one the most important qualities in a new recruit. Are they open-minded to training and self-improvement? Those who are quick studies have a better chance of reaching great success.
2. **S**incerity—Are they believable? Do they sincerely want to be successful? If their wants and desires are high, in most cases you can expect their efforts to be too.
3. **P**ersonality—Remember, people buy from those they like.

There is a big difference between how to view an inexperienced recruit, and how to view the veteran salesperson. Make sure, when looking at a veteran recruit, that they don't have the job-hopper mentality. Every new salesperson means an investment on the part of your company. Are they going to stay long enough to give you a good return on your investment? Observe how eager they are to accept the position. For example, did they accept before hearing all the facts about the job? This might be an indication that they are desperate, and we all know that customers can spot desperation a mile away.

How does the recruit feel about you contacting his or her past employer? I have no problems with coming right out with this question. Be direct—ask them, "Lisa, how do you feel about me contacting your previous employer?" If it is their current employer and they haven't informed them that they are considering a change, that's a different story. However, if they no longer work there and still hesitate when you ask the question, be careful. There may be a problem that you need to investigate.

A common challenge with veteran salespeople is their inflexibility. If you see an inflexible nature as early in the game as during the recruiting process, you can count on it getting worse. Top producing veterans still have to fit into your company culture, yet many have difficulties accepting changes and new rules.

Lastly, if the candidate strongly insists that the income isn't high enough but agrees to accept the job anyway, be on the alert. They may perceive your offer as a stopping off place until something better comes along. That's a manager's nightmare.

> As you look at recruits who job-hop, understand that your superiors may be put off by the number of salespeople who leave your team. They may view your high turnover as an indication that you are a poor recruiter or that there is a significant management problem.

Good recruiting skills can make a big difference in the way the company perceives you as a leader. Some professional leaders are built or broken based on their recruiting abilities.

Recruiting by Ad

Ad responses from the newspaper can be overwhelming. Where you advertise and how your ad reads will determine the type and number of applicants. Establish some ground rules ahead of time, like how many times you want the ad to appear and the length of time you wish the ad to run. Check with your marketing department to see if they have additional cost-saving benefits if you use one paper over another. Make your ads eye-catching and clear. Make the best features of the job prominent in your ad. It helps to ask these two questions:
1. Will my headline attract an applicant's attention?
2. Will that person be the level of recruit I'm looking to have on my team?

> Be sure to give a closing date for accepting applications. Unless you want this to be an ongoing process, let the recruits know there is a deadline that they'll be expected to meet.

Nobody expects professional writing, but the accuracy and salesmanship exhibited by a well-written ad says a lot about you and your company. Proofread your ad. This ad precedes you. If it has several misspelled words or unrelated phrases, this will not be the message you want to leave new recruits. It would be ironic to require someone with strong communication skills and have recruited him or her through an ad that didn't practice what you preached.

The following are samples of a well-written ad that sells and a poorly written one that top producers will skip right over in their search for a position with an exciting, progressive company.

Well-Written Ad that Sells You and Your Company

Are you looking for a lifetime career with limitless income possibilities? Well, we're looking for you, too. If enthusiastic salesperson with strong leadership skills and an eye on upper-management describes you, you're invited to join our team of dedicated professionals. The position requires two years minimal experience in industry or related sales position. Some college is helpful, but an eagerness to learn and a willingness to contribute are essential. Resumes being accepted through March 20th. Respond immediately by sending salary requirements, cover letter and resume to ABC Company, c/o Human Resources Manager, 1111 Northeast Avenue, Glendale, Arizona 85302.

Poorly Written Ad

Need someone immediately! Must have 2 years exp., some college and be a self-starter. We check references. Call John at 404-939-9999.

Even though the first ad would cost a little more to run and take a bit more time to write, I'm sure you can see that it would attract a lot more response from qualified salespeople.

Although using employment agencies or headhunters can be more costly, it can also reduce your paperwork and interviewing time. If that is more important to you, if your time is more valuable than the money paid to an agency, then by all means use them. Going through an agency doesn't necessarily negate your need to further screen them through your human resources department, though.

Whatever you decide, establish a recruitment plan—a processing system.

I would suggest you first set minimal requirements to screen candidate applications. Put one person in charge of telephone applicants, and make someone else responsible for screening the resumes or applications. If you request performance reports or additional materials, assign someone to help you look over those as well. Next, separate candidates into piles. Put all those you'd like to interview in one pile. Have another for possible candidates. After sorting, send a standard letter of appreciation to your rejected candidates and thank them for responding to your ad.

Recruitment Plan Form

Profile of the Ideal Candidate:

Background:

_____

Education Level or Special Training:

_____

Experience:

_____

Personality/Attitude:

_____

Strengths:

_____

Job Description:

_____

_____

Delegated Tasks & Responsible Parties:

_____

_____

_____

_____

_____

Items to Bring to Interview:

_____

Cover Letter/Resume Assessment:

_____

_____

_____

_____

_____

Interview Notes:

_____

_____

_____

_____

_____

_____

_____

_____

_____

_____

Overall Impression:

_____

_____

_____

_____

There are a few things that should be put into practice before you face the challenges of recruiting. Design a form rejection letter; it will save you a great deal of time.

Sample Rejection Letter

DATE
RECRUIT'S NAME
STREET ADDRESS
CITY, STATE ZIP

Dear _____,

I wanted to take a moment to express my appreciation for
the time and effort you put into our interview. Although the
position has been filled, your resume will be kept on file
with us for future consideration.   With your winning
attitude and invaluable experience, I'm sure you'll discover
a good match in your search for a new professional home.

Good luck to you. If I can be of any further assistance,
please don't hesitate to give me a call.

Sincerely,

Thomas Smith
Sales Manager

 Also, prepare your support people who will be
participating in this process.

Let them know ahead of time the traits and qualifications you require to fill the
position. Discuss the type of personality you are looking for as well as the
educational background and special training you want.

Make sure those you choose to help in this process understand the importance of confidentiality. If you are recruiting within the organization, be aware that there are eyes and ears everywhere. An innocent comment or a word in jest can be misunderstood and cause you incredible embarrassment, not to mention the possible discrimination or harassment charges that could develop. Let this be the time when you are at your most professional self.

Vary the Personality Types on Your Sales Team

I'm sure you've all studied the four personality types. It's a good idea to maintain a balance of those personalities on your sales team. The best blend on a team is that which incorporates all four personality types along with a willingness to be versatile and flexible. A team with a majority of members who are driver personalities might be too quick to make decisions and have nobody to carry them out. Too many analytical personalities might delay a project while they discuss every minute detail and consider every possible outcome. A team with too many expressive and amiable personalities will get along famously, but rarely get anything done. They are just too busy having a good time.

> It takes all kinds of salespeople to serve all kinds of customers. Many managers have a tendency to recruit people who are like themselves instead of striving for a balance of personality types.

There is a lot to consider when searching for a good match. Although experience is a great teacher, it also helps to have a recipe for success. This is mine:

> Dilute concentrated preparation with
> five parts positive attitude, three parts
> active listening and two parts follow-
> through. Add a dash of intuition.
> Mix well. Allow time for setup.

Good luck on your recruiting! Adopting these principles will help you make outstanding recruiting the cornerstone for achieving excellent team performance!

Working Through the Process--Chapter Three

❖ Establish a profile for the ideal candidate for your sales team.
One that is for Keeps!

K = Knowledge   How much knowledge do you want your
                                salespeople to have?

_____

_____

E = Experience   How much experience to you expect your
                                salespeople to have?

_____

_____

E = Education   How much education would you like your
                                salespeople to have?

_____

_____

P = Personal Traits   What personal characteristics do you look
                                for in your recruits?

_____

_____

S = Selling Skills   What are the skills you look for in a new
                                recruit?

_____

_____

❖ Eight Ways to Recruit Potentially GREAT Salespeople!

1. Where can you look within your own company?

   _____

   _____

2. What professional connections do you have that you might use as a recruiting source?

   _____

   _____

3. Where can you go for referrals?

   _____

   _____

4. Who worked for you as a top salesperson in the past that you would consider having back again? How could you go about recruiting them?

   _____

   _____

5. What employment services would you consider as a good recruiting source?

   _____

   _____

6. Where would you advertise to find suitable new recruits?

_____

_____

7. Are there any head-hunters in your area who could find you experienced
    top producers? Would the returns be worth your investment?

_____

_____

8. Who do your loyal customers recommend? How would you go about
    recruiting them?

_____

_____

❖ The E.S.P. Signals that Point to Winning Potential in Raw Recruits are...

1. _____ - most important factor.
2. _____ - are the _____?
3. _____ - remember, people ____ from those they ____.
4. _____ _____ - those who are _____ _____ have a better chance
    of reaching _____ _____.
5. _____ - their _____ and _____ are high and so are their _____.
6. _____ - well-groomed and _____.

❖ When Recruiting Experienced Veterans, be Careful...

1. The person is not a ___ _____.

2. That they hear all the _____ about the job before _____.

3. If they ask you not to _____ their _____ _____.

4. If the candidate appears to be _____ at this early stage -- it will only get _____.

5. If the candidate _____ insists his or her _____ isn't high enough, but _____ the job anyway.

❖ Identify your dominant personality style and the personality styles of your people.

Your Personality Style: _____

Dominant Personality Styles of your salespeople: _____

_____

❖ What personality styles would you like to recruit to balance your team? Why?

_____

_____

❖ How would your entire team benefit by creating a better balance?

_____

_____

CHAPTER FOUR
**Interviewing with Your Intellect
As Well As Your Intuition**

 "Many of the things you can count, don't count. Many of the things you can't count, really count."

Albert Einstein

Chapter Highlights:

▶ Updating Your Job Descriptions

▶ Addressing the Cover Letter and Resume

▶ Identifying and Implementing the Three Types of Interviews

▶ Four Stages of an Interview

▶ Arranging and Conducting the Interview

▶ A Commitment to Excellence

The title of this chapter explains a main difference between the way managers and leaders handle the interviewing process. Leaders take the interviewing process a step further than the intellectual management of the situation—they consider the feelings of the candidates and attempt to make the process as pain free as possible.

 A great leader knows what type of person they are looking for to fill the position; they know what skills, attitude and drive that person must possess in order to reach success in the available position. However, they are also intuitive and sensitive to the needs of the new recruit—just as they will expect them to be with customers once they join the team.

Lead with empathy. Don't get that word confused with sympathy. Leaders don't have to feel what their people feel, but rather show intuitive understanding and compassion. It goes back to that old saying that people don't care how much you know until they know how much you care.

> Knowledge, or leading with your intellect, is necessary, but it cannot be at the expense of your intuitive side.

This can often be difficult for some of the veteran managers who have been taught that showing you care is a bit too warm and fuzzy and has no place in the workplace. It's all in your perception. Sometimes you show a person you care by making them get off their backsides and do something productive. I don't think that qualifies as warm and fuzzy, but it certainly could be considered intuitive. In that case, the manager knew the salesperson well enough to understand whether positive or negative motivation would be more effective and was willing to do what it took to help that salesperson reach his or her goals. It took more than knowing (intellect); intuition (feelings) played an important role in that salesperson's success. Being intuitive is often overlooked. It takes a lot more time to develop a relationship with your people in order to understand their feelings and motivations, and time is a leader's most precious commodity.

A manager's job is incredibly busy, and sometimes it requires prioritizing what absolutely has to be completed today and what can be left until tomorrow. One of the things that is continually postponed when you're not in the hiring phase are updated job descriptions. Until you actually have a vacancy, what's the use in updating that position's job description, right? I agree that it doesn't seem too high a priority—that is, until you need it. Then, when you're confronted with the challenges of recruiting, interviewing, weeding through tons of resumes, returning phone calls and sending out rejection letters, nobody has the time to do the job description updates. More importantly, if the person who held the position previously has already left, there may not be anyone who knows the position well enough to update the job description. Then what do you do?

Updating job descriptions doesn't have to take tons of time, especially if there is someone still in the position who has first-hand knowledge of its challenges. Here are a few suggestions to help you work through this process with a minimal amount of effort. When a vacancy occurs, having updated job descriptions will give you and your team a head start.

Job Description Update Suggestions:

Discuss your plans with your assistant and make this his or her special project.

Remember, with special projects you always want to incorporate special rewards.

Make it a worthwhile project, but emphasize that this project can easily be handled in partnership with the person currently in that position.

If you don't already have a "Job Description Update Form" in your files, that will be the first step your assistant will take. If you are without an assistant, your choices are to do it yourself or find some part-time help. We can begin the process as I act as your temporary "fill in" for the job. You may find the following "Job Description Update Form" helpful; it will save you some time. Distribute this form to your team and ask them to complete the form before their next evaluation.

Job Description Update Form

Name:_____

Title:_____

Current Duties:

_____

_____

_____

_____

_____

_____

Duty Changes Since I Took Position:

_____

_____

_____

_____

Extra Requirements Placed On Me Since Accepting this Position:

_____

_____

_____

_____

Additional Training/Education Now Required for Success in this Position:

_____

_____

_____

Challenges of this Position:

_____

_____

_____

_____

Normal Workday Hours: _____

Hours It Takes To Complete Work: _____.

Skills Most Important for the Job:

_____

_____

_____

_____

_____

Character Traits Most Important for the Job:

_____

_____

_____

_____

_____

What are the Most Enjoyable and Rewarding Elements of My Job?

_____

_____

_____

_____

What do affiliates or peers say I do that helps to make their own jobs easier and more productive?

_____

_____

_____

_____

Who Is My Direct Report?

_____

Compare What I Do Now to Previous Job Description on File:

_____

_____

_____

_____

Comments:

_____

_____

_____

_____

_____

Once you or your assistant have gathered the data on ALL your positions, you're ready to begin Phase II of the updating process.

> Be sure to communicate what you are doing in your update so that your people won't feel insecure, suspecting they are being replaced.

Compare what your employees wrote down as their job descriptions with the existing ones in your files. Most likely, you're going to find some glaring differences. Going through this process will be a great exercise for you. It may give you some clues as to why a particular employee is experiencing burnout. Perhaps their job requirements have expanded past the capabilities of one person, and they need HELP!

You won't necessarily have to schedule a meeting with each one of your salespeople and support staff, but as you and your assistant review that employee's evaluation, discuss the updated job description. Be attentive to the position's challenges stated on the updated job descriptions. Assess the evolving changes in the job. Let your salesperson tell you what has been a particular challenge, and what he or she really enjoys about the job. In doing so, you'll get a better idea of what type of person is the best match.

> Think of updating the job description as an investigative process.

You are investigating the aspects of the job that will be appealing to newcomers, and what part of the job will most challenge them. It offers your recruits the ability to make an informed decision about their acceptance or rejection of your offer.

Obviously, this is no overnight venture. In fact, it's an ongoing process that should be repeated every 12-18 months. A lot can change in a position in that time. Territories can change. Quotas can change. Technology will change. Other team members can change who were carrying some of the load of that position, which might mean the current employee will have to pick up the slack. You may want to include on your "Job Description Update Form" an explanation of what the salesperson has been asked to be responsible for in the past 18 months that wasn't within the original job description but was needed to meet a team goal. It's important to know how often those sorts of things occur in the position so you'll know how to plan for the future recruiting needs.

Don't be afraid to ask others in job related departments who work closely with the current employee what could be done that would make their jobs a lot easier. Then ask them what they like most about how the current employee does their job. Perhaps that person is highly organized, or sets the stage well with their customers so there are fewer complaints down the road. Whatever it might be, include those in your updates. Begin working NOW on what could be done better.

Once you work through this process and are able to offer new employees updated job descriptions, you will have started on the right foot. We talked earlier about asking your salespeople to be organized and about teaching by example. Here is your chance to show **your** organizational skills. Let that new employee learn what you expect through your good example.

All this should happen before the interview.

 From designing your ad to communicating what type of candidate you want, few things are more helpful than a CURRENT job description.

If you use an agency for screening or testing, an updated job description is critical. Job descriptions are used to evaluate candidates and inform them of the requirements of the job so that both you and the new employee will be confident and interested in working together. In doing so, you can both be sure you've made the best possible match.

Assessing Cover Letters and Resumes

Let's move on to cover letters and resumes. It's important to spend a few minutes discussing resume and cover letter assessment. Here are a few things to keep in mind when going through your ad responses.

1. Look closely at the cover letter and resume.
   • What overall impression does it give you about the one who sent it?
   • What does it tell you about his or her thoroughness and organizational skills?
   • Does it reveal anything about the candidate's personality?

Don't Forget

Don't allow yourself to be fooled by well-formatted and well-written cover letters and resumes. Unfortunately, things are not always as they appear—including the perceptions you get of candidates through their cover letters and resumes.

Being fooled by the way a person writes reminds me of a story I once heard about Dr. James Murray, the man who took on the task of writing and organizing the Oxford Dictionary in 1933. It was an incredible undertaking, and Dr. Murray soon discovered that he was in desperate need of help on the project.

It wasn't long before another gentleman, Dr. Minors, heard of the challenges Dr. Murray was having in editing the work, so he kindly offered his assistance. Having seen his correspondence and suggestions, Dr. Murray immediately recognized Minors' expertise and solicited his help. Thousands of letters and informational correspondence passed between the two gentlemen, and the project was coming to a close. Dr. Murray's eagerness to meet this generous scholar could be contained no longer, so he extended an invitation for Dr. Minors to stay a week at Oxford University.

Dr. Minors regretfully declined, stating that it was physically impossible for him to accept, but that he would love Dr. Murray to visit him instead. Dr. Murray agreed, never dreaming that his visit would lead him to the Broadmoore Asylum for the Criminally Insane where Dr. Minors was incarcerated as a convicted murderer. Who would have dreamed the scholarly, generous man evidenced by his willingness to help and his articulate and brilliant additions to the Oxford Dictionary was a mad-dog murderer? You see; things are not always as they appear.

2. Note the specific points of interest in the cover letter and on the resume.
   • Do the facts show any inconsistent issues?
   • What are the applicant's areas of expertise?
   • How will these work within the culture of your sales team?

3. Does this particular applicant's qualifications meet the requirements of your job description? Give the cover letter and resume an overall rating, perhaps from 1-10. Would you want to see a report delivered with an equal amount of care and thoroughness? If not, remember what we said about organizational skills. It's only going to get worse.

Once you have established the recruitment process, and taken a look at the cover letters and resumes, now is the time to decide a processing strategy. This will determine the type of interview you plan. Let's review a few different interviewing types and styles in order for you to determine which one best fits your situation and management methods.

> Vary the type of interviews conducted to see how your candidate responds in different situations.

Types of Interviews

The Preliminary or Screening Interview

This type of interview does just what it says—it narrows the field. It is typically used to decide who goes further and who is not suited for the job. This interview type is short and based more on fact-finding than situational problem solving.

Second Interview

This interview is more probing, seeking detailed information the manager will need to determine a good match between the newcomer and his or her sales team. They are typically 1 ½ to 2 hours in length. You may have the candidate meet several members on the team and then solicit their responses. During the second interview, you'll want the candidate to meet his or her direct report.

Panel or Group Interview

In this type of interview gather several group leaders and supervisors to share in the interviewing process. One thing to be cautious about in a panel or group interview—you may not see as much of the candidate's personality. In this situation, it is quite stressful for the one being interviewed.

> To decrease the tension in a panel or group interview, hold it off site in a more relaxed atmosphere like a restaurant or resort.

You will definitely get a clear idea of how the candidate responds to high-pressure situations. A suggestion: wear nametags, or if held in a conference room, give the candidate your cards and then get up for coffee or a drink of water. This will give the candidate a little time to place your name with your face. Then he or she will be able to refer to you by name. You can also use this situation to determine the candidate's resourcefulness.

Each manager has his or her own particular style, or method of discovering information about the candidate. What is your style? Do you prefer a question and answer style that is highly structured? Or is your style less formal, focusing on discoveries made about candidates' skills, while at the same time making them comfortable enough to allow their personalities to shine through? Some managers like to ask stressful questions and pin a candidate to the wall to see how he or she will react in difficult situations. If that is more your style, reserve it for the second interview. There is no use subjecting candidates whom you have no intention of hiring to that process.

Four Basic Stages of an Interview

 No matter what particular style you use, every well-planned interview will go through four basic stages: the introduction, the discovery process, the focus and the close.

Let me explain what should ideally happen in each stage.

Introduction

Begin with some small talk. Allow your candidate to ask some casual questions and you do the same. The purpose of this stage of the interview is to create a relaxed atmosphere and a comfortable level of communication.

The Discovery Process

At this point, shift the small talk into a phase of gathering general information. It's also a time when you tell candidates about your company's philosophy and vision. With preparation and skill, you can discover just how well candidates have done their homework. How much do they know about your company? Listen to the questions they ask. Do they indicate an organized, well-prepared candidate? If so, this could be a reflection of how they will perform on the job.

This is also a time to discover the candidate's goals. Do some things in the discovery process that will test listening and observation skills. During this stage, you'll get a good idea of individual personality, confidence level and personal aspirations. Then ask yourself, is this the kind of person I would like on my team of professionals?

The Focus

This is when the manager begins to focus or concentrate on the job and how the candidate might fit in with his or her team. Give the candidate an opportunity to demonstrate his or her skills. This should be the time to FOCUS on the candidate not on the company requirements.

The Close

At this stage, you should summarize what has been said and clarify certain points you've both established. Be sure you have made the proper notations on your "Interview Review Form." By the way, if you don't have one, this is another item you or your assistant will need to design. Ask the candidate during the close if he or she has anything else to add, or any additional questions you have not covered. Learn from the questions applicants ask. Let their questions be a tool of measurement as to what he or she has already researched about your company and how well the candidate listened and observed during the interview.

Now it's time for you to enter into the selection phase of the interviewing process. Who will be chosen for the interview? From the many applications, in most cases there are only a small number of candidates who will be suitable for consideration.

When you have narrowed the field, administer any tests this position might require in order to filter through possible recruits.

> Make sure that you do a good job of narrowing. Interviewing too many candidates will not only eat up your time but will confuse the selection process.

It's like looking for a new home; if you look at too many houses in one day, pretty soon they all begin to look the same.

After you've looked through the resumes, give the pile of rejected applicants to your secretary. Get a head start on contacting them, and they'll appreciate your prompt response so they can continue their job search. I can't stress to you enough how important it is to use a courteous and professional manner. If at all possible, write thank you notes that will add one little personal touch to each rejection letter. Encourage them.

> Leave them with a good feeling about you and your company—even if they weren't considered for the position.

Who knows, they might not be right for that particular position but be a perfect match for another opening down the road. Leave your options open.

There are some logistical issues to consider that will play a very important part in setting the tone for the interview. This is the phase where you ARRANGE the interview. First of all, give applicants time to set their schedules and cover their bases. Then they won't be distracted by worry or tension, feeling like they need to rush back to their jobs or other obligations.

Points to Remember When ARRANGING the Interview

1. Avoid all interruptions during the interview. Shut off your mobile phone and put your pager on vibrate. Ask your assistant to hold your calls or let your voice mail take messages for you, and put a "Do Not Disturb" sign on your door.
2. Be rested and alert for the interview. Going through the interviewing process can be exhausting. Make sure you do everything possible to keep your energy level high.
3. Allow enough time between appointments so that the interviewees won't bump into their competition outside your door.
4. Give yourself time to write detailed notes after each interview.
5. Choose a location with comfortable seating, balanced climate and adequate lighting.

Conducting the Interview

Now let's examine how to actually conduct the interview. If you have set the stage for a proper interview, it's time to make all that work pay off. If your style of interviewing is more formal, it's okay to sit behind your desk. However, if your style is conversational, easy—then come out from behind your desk and sit at a round table in your office or side-by-side in comfortable chairs. This will make the candidate feel much more comfortable.

Watch your body language and your expressions in response to things the candidate says. You'd be surprised at what you might give away by your automatic reactions. You don't want to influence answers because you indicated your like or dislike of the candidate's response. Make eye contact often, and be attentive to whether the applicant does the same. It can give you a clue as to their confidence level. Avoid asking personal questions that are irrelevant to the job. And, offer positive feedback to encourage more discussion. When they answer a question candidly, show them respect for doing so. Showing your acceptance of their honest responses will encourage them to offer more of the same.

Lastly, don't forget to thank them for their time in the interview.

| Don't Forget | Remember what I said about making them feel good about your company. Even if you have decided they won't make a good fit for this particular position, show them the respect and courtesy they deserve. |

You never know who they might know.

For some managers, the interview process comes naturally. For other managers, interviewing is a tedious, uncomfortable process that brings a sigh of relief when it's over. If it's natural for you, you may not need a list of questions— you're better going off the cuff. However, if it is awkward for you to question a candidate about their background or experience, to ask them questions that would reveal their strong and weak personality traits, then you may want to refer to a questions list during the interview.

Do this anyway. Then you'll ask the same general questions of every candidate. When you are ready to compare responses, you will be comparing apples to apples.

Suggested Questions to Include in the Interview

1. Why do you want to change jobs?
2. What do you consider your greatest attribute?
3. What have your relationships been like with past employers?
4. What has been your career highlight so far?
5. What has been your career low point so far?
6. What experience do you have problem solving?
7. What additional training and/or education do you have in sales?
8. What are your long-term goals? How do you think you can achieve them with our company?

NOTE: If you want to challenge them and discover how well they have prepared for the interview, move on to the tougher questions. However, most managers reserve those types of questions for the second interview.

Second Interview Question Suggestions

1. What do you believe would be most interesting about working with our company?
2. Which one of our products or services do you think will be the easiest for you to sell, based on your style and skills?
3. Can you demonstrate the selling sequence as if I am a client and you are the salesperson representing our company? That is a tough one, but it will let you know what the candidate is made of.
4. What in our ad attracted you to apply for the position?
5. What has your research shown you about our growth potential and our company culture?
6. Having listened to what I told you about our company and the team I manage, what do you feel you could successfully contribute to the team?
7. Close your eyes. Now, based on what you've seen in my office, can you tell me something about my family or my hobbies? (This will let you know the strength of observation skills.)

Those are tough questions. If your style is tough, and you really want to separate the gutsy from the timid, use them. You'll either scare them off, or they'll appreciate the opportunity to strut their stuff.

If it is the final interview and you realize you want the candidate to become a part of your team, get a commitment from him or her right away. Offer a personal commitment in order to let the candidate know you'll work your hardest to make sure he or she grows and develops into one of your top producers. The following are some questions to ask that will move you to the commitment:

Manager: You told me, Julie, that you decided to leave your last job because of give their reason here.)

Salesperson: That's right.

Manager: What would you say if I made a commitment to you to help you never to have to fall back on that type of job again?

Salesperson: I'd say that sounds great!

Manager: What do you say we work together and commit your goals to paper. What would you like your first year's income to be with our company?

Salesperson: $80,000

Manager: Okay, broken down into quarters, that would be about $20,000 every 90 days, correct.

Salesperson: That sounds about right.

Manager: Breaking it down every month, that would make it roughly a little less than $7,000 per month, right?

Salesperson: That's right.

Manager: Okay, we've talked about your financial goals—now what about your personal goals.

Salesperson: I'd like a new computer.

Manager: Good. And, what about your family goals?

Salesperson: Well, we've been wanting to take a vacation.

Manager: Let me ask you, Julie, are you serious about reaching these goals?

Salesperson: Absolutely!

Manager: Are you ready to commit to doing whatever it takes to achieve these goals?

Salesperson: Yes, I am.

Manager: Good. Because of your commitment, I too am willing to make a personal commitment to do whatever it takes to help you reach those goals. In order for me to do that,

I'd like your permission to make special requirements of you now and again, if necessary, to keep you on track.

Salesperson: You have my permission.

Manager: Great!   Let's put all that we've spoken of today in writing, shall we?

NOTE: Make sure both of you authorize the agreement and then tuck it in the new recruit's file to be reviewed quarterly.

Manager's Commitment to Excellence

As manager, I commit to do whatever it takes to help

_____

accomplish the goals set forth in our conversation on

_____

Approve _____

Salesperson's Commitment to Excellence

As salesperson, I commit to let

_____

do whatever it takes to assist me in the accomplishment of my goals. Since I believe my success is dependent upon our team efforts, I promise to do my part, such as: be punctual, attend meetings, keep a positive attitude and avoid pettiness and negative thinking. If I, for any reason, refuse or am unable to live up to my commitment, I welcome and expect the advice and counsel of

_____

to help reinforce and refocus on my goals.

Approve _____

Beware! There are some topics you should definitely avoid.

For example, it is illegal for an employer to ask questions during the interviewing process that are of a personal nature. You can't ask if they are married or single, if they have children or belong to a certain religious group. And, those things should really have no bearing on whether or not they will make a great addition to your team.

There are even some illegal aspects to questions that refer to national origin, race/color, age, citizenship, disability or criminal record. Every state is different, so I can't speak for the state in which you live and work. But some states have laws about drug testing as well. I've even heard of companies who have mandatory drug testing requirements in states where it is illegal. These companies are usually national firms, and their district or regional managers haven't bothered to discover whether or not they are in compliance with their state laws.

If your policy and procedural manual has an "all managers must" section, be sure that what they require of you is legal. If push comes to shove, you are ultimately responsible for what goes on in that interview—no matter what your manual states that all managers must do.

Although it is not illegal, I would suggest you steer clear of political issues. Politics have no place in an interview unless you're running for office and hiring a campaign manager or speech writer. Whatever isn't relevant to the job is just conversation, and with your busy schedule—do you have time for that?

Let the candidate know when you'll be closing the interviewing process and making your decision. Tell them when you'll be contacting them, and by what method: phone call or letter. Also, you may want to ask them, should they be selected, when it would be possible for them to start.

Most importantly, throughout the interviewing process—BE HONEST! Don't try to paint an incredible picture of your company if you are going through a tough transitional period. If this is a candidate that you are interested in hiring, they will know the truth of the matter soon enough. BE HONEST! If the candidate's salary requirements are too high but you think he or she is a strong candidate, say so—BE HONEST! When considering candidates, if you have concerns about anything on their resume, ask them clarifying questions!

Don't Forget

You just can't afford not to be honest with them—and what you need from them is honesty as well. Remember; you set the stage for a well-planned, successful interview.

Working Through the Process--Chapter Four

❖ What are six things you do to help you prepare for an interview?

1. _____

2. _____

3. _____

4. _____

5. _____

6. _____

❖ What will you add to or omit from the above list of preparations? Why?
Additional Preparations:

_____

_____

Unnecessary Preparations:

_____

_____

❖ When reviewing a candidate's resume, how will you handle...
Inconsistencies?

_____

Gaps:

_____

Over/Under Qualifications:

_____

Mistakes or Errors:

_____

False or Unverifiable Statements:

_____

❖ How will you establish the following for an interview?

Scheduling Appointments:

_____

Location:

_____

Seating Arrangements:

_____

Tone:

_____

❖ Important Points to Remember When Arranging Interviews
   1. Give applicants _____ to _____ the interview.
   2. _____ _____ during the interview.
   3. Be _____ and _____ for the interview.
   4. Make _____ _____ in case trainees are unable to _____.

5. Allow enough time between interviews so that interviewees won't _____ into their _____ outside the door.

6. Give yourself time to _____ _____ _____ after each interview.

7. Choose a place that will be relatively _____ of _____.

8. Choose a location with _____ _____, balanced _____ and adequate _____.

❖ What questions have you asked in the past that you will not continue to ask in the future?

_____

_____

_____

_____

❖ What questions will you add to gather additional information?

_____

_____

_____

_____

❖ Suggested Questions for Applicant
1. Why do you want to make a _____?
2. What do you consider your _____ _____?
3. What have your _____ been like with _____ employers?
4. What has been your _____ _____ to date?
5. What has been your _____ _____ to date?

6. What experience do you have _____ _____?

7. What additional _____ and/or _____ do you have in sales?

8. What are your _____ _____? How do you think you can _____ them by joining our team of professionals?

❖ How will you notify the people you do not choose? How does this differ from the method you used in the past?

_____

_____

_____

_____

❖ Interviewing Strategies

1. _____-- get _____ information. Candidates _____ is less important in this strategy.

2. _____--see how the candidate _____ some key _____ that could be encountered in this _____.

3. _____--see how the applicant will be able to _____ _____.

4. _____--determine if candidate has the _____ skills.

CHAPTER FIVE
Encouraging the MAVERICK Thinker

"'Caution! The left-brained world wants you to 'be realistic'... 'quit dreaming'... 'get your head out of the clouds'... 'get your feet on the ground'... and 'be just like us.' To advance and prosper, steadfastly ignore that advice.'"

Marilyn Grey

Chapter Highlights:

▶ Identifying Your MAVERICK Thinkers
▶ The Value of MAVERICKS
▶ Encouraging Your MAVERICKS to Become Masters
▶ The Three "C's" of Outstanding Team Development
▶ A Balance Between MAVERICK and Traditional Thinkers

Every giant leap in your industry; every major change in your department; every sizeable step in the personal development of someone on your sales team was most likely heavily influenced by a "Maverick" thinker. Mavericks are catalysts for change, and they promote individuality and appreciate the differences of their co-workers. Why? Because they know what it's like to be a step outside the circle. They know how it feels to have ideas that are discarded because they are so far ahead of their time. They understand the true power of seeing things from the other side—the opposite perspective.

Take a look at your salespeople. Do you manage a few Mavericks? How are Maverick thinkers received by you and your team? Many managers inhibit the Maverick's ability to bring about innovative, imaginative, positive changes within the organization because the managers are unaware of the value of their Maverick thinkers.

You'll know the Mavericks because they are the ones who are considered loners or the "problem child" of the department—often perceived to be high-maintenance employees. Mavericks tend to roam from department to department, from organization to organization, seldom appreciated or valued for their input—ironically, that would be the best reward you could ever offer them.

> If the Mavericks of this world were given voice and valued for their input, we probably would have enjoyed many more creative inventions, maintained an incredible lead in technological advancement, and out distanced the world in the production and distribution of goods and services.

In fact, the United States was considered the leader in all these areas at one time—and guess what, that was when we valued Maverick thinkers.

When thinking outside the box was welcomed and appreciated, we had Mavericks by the millions. Our country was explored and populated by Mavericks—and we prospered because of them. But let's reduce this to the importance of the Maverick to corporate America. In fact, let's take a look into the culture of your very own company. What can valuing your Maverick thinkers get you and your company?

The Benefit of Valuing Your Maverick Thinkers

The Maverick thinker can put you heads and shoulders above your competition. Remember what I said about Mavericks being wanderers? Well, if you have a veteran salesperson who, over the years, has moved from company to company, it could be he or she never felt appreciated. During the years when these Mavericks were on the move, though, they gained some extensive knowledge of how your competitors operate and manage their sales team.

The Mavericks probably know your competition better than anyone else in your company. They've lived there; they've had a hand in developing your competitor's concepts and ideas; they were probably the ones who pushed for innovation and change. All that information about all those different companies they've been a part of is still stored in their heads. They carry with them a warehouse of product knowledge, negative and positive end results from creative strategies, and all the "could have been" concepts from these powerful gatherings that never made it past the drawing board.

They can open your eyes to the full impact of your decisions—good or bad. Give them a voice in your meetings and they'll usually play the part of the devil's advocate. Sometimes they're a regular pain in the backsides when you want to move forward on an idea that everybody else on the team has blessed. Why? Because the Maverick will see the bigger picture and point out some real stumbling blocks along the way. Most of the time they just wear people out, and so they give up on trying to share their concerns. Consequently, they let you make the mistakes they see you destined to make.

Wouldn't it have been a better idea to take the time to listen to the concerns of the Maverick? What if they could have saved you a lot of money and time down the road? What if, by being patient in the beginning, you would have been able to resolve issues that ended up causing a failed project? Instead, many managers and members of their teams cop an attitude of "Well, there goes Ted again. He just can't resist putting down our ideas."

Unfortunately, Mavericks have been put down themselves so much that they don't have a lot of tact when it comes to expressing their different viewpoints. They often blurt out their opinions at inappropriate times, and all the other salespeople roll their eyes or click their tongues in disgust. Or, they hold it in for as long as they can, until finally their beliefs burst forward in complaints or impatience when they see that things are being incorrectly implemented. Consequently, they are seen as complainers instead of contributors.

Mavericks can keep you from setting and achieving unnecessary goals because they see that bigger picture. One stage that you want your Mavericks to feel safe in is during the planning process of any project.

- If you encourage them, and believe in them, they will help your team to anticipate the challenges of your endeavor and lead the way to overcoming those challenges.
- If your goals are out of alignment with company goals and objectives, they'll be the first to see it coming.
- If your goals are too low, they'll help your team expand its vision.
- If they are too high, they'll challenge your team with all the negatives with which it will be bombarded.

Can you see now why few Mavericks are appreciated? No matter which way they turn, they seem to always be throwing a monkey wrench into the works.

As a leader, you never have to suffer through the antics of this "problem child." That's right. You can choose to stifle their innovation, to cloud their vision and refuse their voice in improving your team. You can do that, and you'll never have to defend them, explain away their tactless behavior or comments, or act as arbitrator to the conflict they often stir up. What will it cost you? If it means forfeiting your Mavericks, I'd say, the price is too high!

Recognizing Maverick Thinkers

How can you recognize a true Maverick thinker? Are they the ones who always play devil's advocate and speak out their opposition? Although I may have given you that impression, that won't be the case with veteran Maverick thinkers. Those who have a history of rejection and demotivating leadership may have learned by this time to keep their mouths shut. So, you may have Mavericks who sit back in the corner of the meeting and never offer one comment. They hesitate to speak, even when invited to do so by their peers.

Don't let their behavior fool you. They have keen observation and listening skills that keep them well informed of every issue. For all those meetings when they never speak out, they have carefully stored the information. They also have very keen memories! They remember the negatives slung their way, and that is what often keeps them from contributing. They also remember all the ideas and strategies they believed would have worked, and they can be ready with those ideas at the drop of a hat, if encouraged.

Your Mavericks might not be veterans, however. What if this is the first experience they have in sales? They could be new kids on the block, fearless of those staid, traditional thinkers. If so, these young pups will often be loud and appear to be over-zealous. Some of your veteran salespeople will take the time to listen to their ideas, but for the most part, they'll be ignored or teased for their outlandish suggestions. Pretty soon, they go the way of most Mavericks and discover new outlets for all that energy. Maybe they are the ones who seek their thrills in driving that "hot" little sports car. Or, they create diversions for themselves by taking up hobbies like skydiving or drag racing. Some will leave the company to venture out as entrepreneurs, feeling it's their only hope for creativity in their work.

Some ways to spot the Mavericks are these:

1. They are usually the ones to receive all the current trade journals or trade magazines of your industry. Because many of them are loners, you'll see them curled up with one over a sandwich at their desk during lunch.

2. Or, they may be the ones who walk during their lunch hour, plugged in to those irritating headphones. You might think they are listening to music, but, in reality, they are listening to their favorite sales trainer or motivational speaker. Their challenge is to hear others that think like them; someone who values their differences; who can relate to their need to express and develop creative strategies.

3. Spotting the Mavericks in a meeting isn't too difficult. Even if they are quiet, you can bank on one thing with veteran Mavericks. They so rarely offer input anymore unless others insist, that when they do speak up people tend to listen. It's like E. F. Hutton—the world listens. Even when other members of your team expect the bomb of negative to hit, they still listen.

> When others get stuck for new ideas, they will automatically go to the Maverick. They may not like what he or she has to say, but pretty soon what is brought to the well is a bucket brimming with new ideas and welcomed, progressive strategies.

One of the most difficult things for Mavericks is that they constantly face and oppose the traditional thoughts of upper management. Mavericks rarely get into upper management. Why? Well, think about it. They are loners—not conducive to being promoted in a corporate environment that values **who** you know rather than **what** you know.

> They aren't usually promoted for their winning personalities. Unless the founder of the company was a Maverick, you won't find too many of his or her right-handers who think differently, either. They just aren't "YES" people.

It really is your responsibility to draw out the contributions of your Mavericks. Set the tone of your meetings and create a safe environment in which everyone is encouraged to participate.

Who are your Mavericks? Make it a habit to listen, not just hear, but truly listen, to your people and the Mavericks will soon make themselves heard. If everyone feels valued for their knowledge and expertise, it won't be long before others will start offering your Mavericks their just rewards. Their ideas will be considered. They will be invited to give opposing views. In fact, your team will see Mavericks as people who can anticipate challenges before they block the team's progressive movement toward the successful achievement of its goals.

Profile of a Maverick

By now you should be getting a picture of what I mean by Maverick thinkers. However, if you still have some doubts let me take it a step further!

- Maverick thinkers are those who see things a bit differently. You might say they dance to a different tune or march to a different drummer than most people in your organization.

- Mavericks are happiest when they aren't made to conform. They often just don't understand why their behavior or thinking is considered unacceptable to others.

One great thing about Mavericks—they allow others to freely express and they appreciate creative differences.

- Mavericks have been taught very expensive lessons. Those lessons have made them sensitive to rejection. They've been taught that many managers don't appreciate someone who doesn't agree with them. They've been taught the pain of isolation because team members consider them to be troublemakers—complainers. They've been taught that sometimes the only way to find satisfaction in their job is to go into business for themselves. Our companies are losing those wonderfully creative thinkers. Consequently, we're losing our edge in the global marketplace.

Encouraging Your Mavericks to Become Masters

How can you encourage Maverick thinkers in your organization? If you believe what I've said and feel they can bring great value to your company, you'll want to protect your Mavericks. If you've listened to what I've indicated are the Mavericks' special challenges, you'll already have some ideas of your own brewing. If one of the strongest motivations for Mavericks is to be appreciated, who better to do that than Maverick managers?

> Once you've identified your Mavericks and recognized the many contributions they could make to your team, give them opportunities to band together with other Mavericks.

You won't want to do this in every meeting; it could be quite chaotic. What you could do is set up a "think tank" for those who need to share ideas that might be far before their time. Get them together. Provide a meeting place or retreat for them to express concepts or ideas for product development, or even new methods of sales and distribution. Who knows, you could lead your company to be first in the development of a new strategy, service or product that will make it millions and you a hero. Now, that's worth giving the Mavericks voice, isn't it?

As a leader of Mavericks, it is especially important for you to keep your word, for you to support their issues.

Remember, they've been beat up in organizations quite a bit, and they need to know you are not a clone of others who paid them lip service in the past.

When you provide this "think tank" environment, find at least one idea you can support. Encourage them to take the idea and design a plan of action that will move their idea forward. Make them feel safe that if it fails, they will just return to the drawing boards. The following are some suggestions when dealing with Mavericks:

1. Be honest in your communications.
2. Be open in your thoughts.
3. Be welcoming and receptive to new ideas.
4. Be willing to reward contributions that prove to be profitable and productive, no matter how different they might sound at first.
5. Be ready to support them, helping them to fight against the negatives they may get from traditional thinkers.
6. Be respectful of their feelings when you do have to go against their suggestions.
7. Be dependable and loyal to the project; let them know you appreciate their insight.
8. Be consistent, focused on a philosophy that allows every team member to feel safe in offering his or her own expertise.
9. Be determined to ACT on the suggestions you feel are good.
10. Be discerning, knowing when to continue and when to back off.

Some of the greatest managers are Mavericks that have learned to play the game.

They've learned to maintain their creativity while at the same time conform to some of the ideas of traditional thought. A great thing about giving your Mavericks a voice on your team—you get to have a little fun yourself.

Evaluating Your Mavericks' Efforts

Along with the new concepts and ideas, new strategies and information Mavericks bring to the table, as a manager you will need to create a whole new system of measurement. Evaluating the Maverick can be difficult. The rewards and incentives for them are usually not linked to higher commissions or increased base pays. Instead, Mavericks are rewarded by things like "think tanks" with other Mavericks. They are encouraged by your unwavering support. That's why, even when you believe an idea to be so "out there" that it borders on the ridiculous, let them begin acting to implement their ideas. Mavericks are very intelligent, and one in the group will soon see the foolishness of their ways, back up, and move toward a modified goal that could make an incredible contribution to the team. Be patient with them, and encourage them to be patient with themselves.

Attracting the Maverick

> There is a universal law of attraction. It states that like attracts like, so the best way to attract the Maverick thinker is to be one.

When you have a great idea, don't be afraid to take it to the board or your CEO. If they shoot you all sorts of negatives, listen to their concerns, take into consideration how their concerns will mean changing your idea, make the necessary changes, then take the modifications back to them.

You were given your position of leader for a purpose—not only to fulfill your own chosen path, but to also forge the way for your people to do the same. One of the ways you can do this is to value the form of communications that is most neglected: good listening! Hear the concerns of your team members. Then take it a step further. Actually listen with the mindset that you will be "moved to act" or motivated to implement their ideas. Sure, you may need to modify them, calm them down a bit, or some you'll have to discard altogether. Whatever the case may be, leave Mavericks feeling good about their abilities to create, and encourage them to continue the creative flow.

Adopt the mindset that you can do anything in which you focus your thought and energy. The greater the number who focus on the same thing, the more powerful and far reaching that endeavor will be.

Remember this; if you expect your team to be creative and share their creativity with you and the rest of the team, you will need to teach by example.

When you are willing to make yourself vulnerable, your team will do the same. Practice the 3 **C**s with your team:

1. Have the **C**OURAGE to be creative, different and original in your management style. Expect those you serve to do the same in their sales careers.
2. Have the **C**ONFIDENCE to share those things with your people, and offer them the help they need to build their own confidence levels.
3. Be **C**ONSIDERATE of those on your team who may have had to suffer challenges in the past because they were Maverick thinkers. Let them know you appreciate their willingness to take those calculated risks for the good of the team.

Keeping A Balance

There is a balance to all this.

> In the process of appreciating your Mavericks, don't discard your steady, traditional thinkers.

If some of your salespeople are doing the fundamentals better than almost anyone you have, recognize their efforts. Don't devalue traditional thinkers because you are trying to build an inspiring team of creative individuals. Keep a balance!

Balance is everything. It takes all kinds to ensure successful operations. There is no place for put downs, by yourself or anyone else. As a manager, it's important that you don't play favorites. Let me tell you why. Not only will others begin to discount your pet salespeople's input because they believe their ideas are accepted more for who they know than what they know—but because it creates imbalance on your team.

When you take someone into your confidences, you can bet that it will take a whole 60 seconds from the time they leave your office for what you said in confidence to be spread to every ear in your organization. If you feel the need to maintain confidences, do so with that thought in mind. In other words, say how much you value Cindy for her consistent, solid and insightful contributions to the team. Make sure you tell your confidant, I wouldn't want this to get out for fear people will think I favor the girl, but Cindy has brought great dimension to our team. You can set your clock by it—about one minute later, Cindy is hearing what was said about her. Do the same with everybody.

Have you ever noticed when you think you aren't supposed to hear something, you're straining yourself to catch every precious word. I once had a friend who called her pediatrician because she couldn't get her four-year-old to listen. The pediatrician told her to whisper. Sure enough, it worked so well, that to this day, when she wants to make sure her 28-year-old son is listening to her, she whispers.

The same is true with you and your salespeople. Don't just select a few to pass the word, to have your confidence. Let them all join the fun. At one time or another, take them one-by-one into your confidences. Then step back and observe the affect of all that positive input. It's so much more productive than asking another salesperson, "What the heck is Jeff up to? I never see him do one thing toward contributing to the team." Wouldn't it be much more effective to say, "You know, even though Jeff chooses to keep to himself, I have really noticed his ability to listen and observe everything around him, haven't you?" Before you know it, all that positive will come back to you. Your confidant will repeat what you said, on total accident of course. Then that person will tell another and another, and pretty soon you have a snowball of positive appreciation, picking up momentum as it rolls downhill.

What to Expect

Look out! The word's getting out that you and your team have some pretty strong Maverick thinkers. When more traditional managers treat you with less respect because they see your ideas as "out there," the best thing to do is practice some of the following:

- Keep offering your insights, and enjoying the privilege of being known as progressive thinkers. Don't let their regards for your suggestions keep you from contributing.
- Refuse to judge them because of their lack of imagination and creativity. Wouldn't that be as bad as their judgment against you? Know that it takes all kinds to make a well-balanced company. It takes the traditional thinking managers as well as the Mavericks.
- Keep appreciating the talents of traditional thinkers as well. It's usually their stable, proven strategies that anchor your innovative ones to sound techniques and methodologies.
- Include them in the planning stages of your Maverick projects. Ask their advice, then take it. It will give your project more stability and offer more popularity when you are ready to present it to the company big wigs.
- Most importantly, be an equal opportunity manager.

> If you have done your homework, you've created a great team with differing personality styles, different thinkers and different expertise. Use and appreciate them all!

From one Maverick manager to another, let me share with you how doing these things benefited me in return. When I listened to traditional thinkers but was still able to follow my dreams, I pursued my career with the confidence that I was using proven techniques and strategies. I developed the courage to put my own personal twist on things and perhaps reach those of you who haven't been touched by the more traditional educators. Being a Maverick earned me the position of top salesperson, top manager, top owner, award winning performer, and now it has earned me the privilege to do what I love most. Being a Maverick has provided me the opportunity to speak to some of you Mavericks out there who are facing the same struggles I faced, and who need some encouragement and direction. I want you to know, all you Maverick managers, that you are definitely in good company. Keep up the innovative work!

Working Through the Process--Chapter Five

❖ What is a MAVERICK thinker?

1. One who often see things _____ from the commonly _____ norm.
2. Maverick thinkers are _____ when they aren't made to _____ to what others consider acceptable _____ or _____.
3. Mavericks can often appear to be _____ and/or _____ because they've been taught to keep their _____ to themselves.
4. Maverick thinkers could be _____ information that could make an _____ _____ to the team--so _____ the _____ to participate.
5. Maverick thinkers are usually _____ _____. They know what it's like not being _____ by being given the _____ to freely express.

❖ Identify at least three MAVERICK thinkers you have on your team. What makes them MAVERICKS?

1. _____

2. _____

3. _____

❖ How are your MAVERICK thinkers perceived by their peers?   Upper management?

Peers:

_____

Upper Management:

_____

❖ List at least five ways your MAVERICK thinkers have contributed to your sales team.

1. _____

2. _____

3. _____

4. _____

5. _____

❖ What special challenges do your MAVERICK thinkers present?

_____

_____

❖ Do you consider yourself to be somewhat of a MAVERICK thinker? Explain!

_____

_____

❖ How has the MAVERICK within yo influenced your sales team?

_____

_____

❖ After reading this chapter, list at least five ways you can value your MAVERICK thinkers.

1. _____

2. _____

3. _____

4. _____

5. _____

❖ Ten Ways to Encourage the Maverick Thinkers
  1. Be _____ in your _____.
  2. Be _____ in your _____.
  3. Be _____ and _____ to new ideas.
  4. Be _____ to _____ contributions that prove to be _____ and
     _____.
  5. Be _____ to _____ them, helping them to fight against the
     _____ they may get from _____ thinkers.
  6. Be _____ of their _____ when you do have to _____
     with their suggestions.
  7. Be _____ and _____ to the project; let them know you
     _____ their _____.
  8. Be _____, focused on a _____ that allows every team
     member to feel _____ offering their _____.
  9. Be _____ to ___ on the suggestions you feel are good.
  10. Be _____, knowing when to continue to analyze and when to
      move on.

❖ In order to value your MAVERICK thinkers, what changes will this require
  in your management style and methods?

  _____

  _____

  _____

CHAPTER SIX
Becoming A Powerful Decision Maker

"There is nothing more to be esteemed than a manly firmness and decision of character. I like a person who knows his own mind and sticks to it; who sees at once what, in given circumstances, is to be done, and does it."

William Hazlitt

Chapter Highlights:

▶ A Step-by-Step Decision-Making Process
▶ Methods & Styles of Decision Making
▶ Tips for Better Decision Making
▶ Barriers to Decision Making
▶ Making those Tough Decisions
▶ Intuitive vs. Logical Decision Making
▶ Taking Massive Action

When you define the word "decision," it sounds simple, really.

A decision is merely a choice among alternative courses of action.

How will you deal with the problem? Many managers make decisions by comparing different choices, but their challenges are that they are often uninformed, haven't gathered enough knowledge to make an informed decision, or have a limited vision of opposing factors that could heavily influence the outcomes of those decisions. Suddenly—things get a lot more complicated. That's why I wanted to spend this chapter with you discussing decision making.

Decision Making Processes

1. <u>Identification</u> = What exactly has to be decided, and how is this decision best made?
2. <u>Analysis</u> = What are your alternatives?
3. <u>Assessment</u> = What are the pros and cons of each viable option?
4. <u>Choice</u> = Which alternative do you believe to be the best?
5. <u>Planning</u> = What action needs to be taken, by whom, and when should we expect results?

Defining the Problem—Discovering the Options

To arrive at a decision, managers will need to first define the purpose of the action. What has brought things to a head? While that may sound like an easy task, sometimes a manager knows there is a problem, but can't identify it. We're not especially trained to do that. Most of the time, in our high school and university studies we are given the problem and asked to find viable solutions to that problem. We send out thousands of graduates with great strengths in problem solving, but not in problem identification. So, first on your agenda is to identify. Once you know what the problem is, it will be much easier to get to the root of the matter.

The next step, listing all the available options, also sounds easy, doesn't it? After all, if you know the problem, then isn't it a logical progression just to gather all the information and people together and have a big brainstorming session until the problem is resolved? While brainstorming is great in theory, it is much more difficult in practical application. There are so many steps to decision making and numerous barriers to your success as a decision-maker, that I thought it would be helpful to take it one step at a time. That's the way you'll need to resolve your challenges—one step at a time.

When you have identified the problem, your first inclination is to quickly gather all the information you'll need to make the decision, then make it and get on with other things. However, some decisions require a lot more insight than that. If not given the proper attention, a quick decision can give rise to many, many more problems down the road. You cannot gather the necessary materials to make an informed decision until you have identified who the contributors of that material should be.

For example, you may be the only one involved in making the final decision, but within that decision-making process you'll have many helpers. Keep in mind that the ultimate responsibility will be yours, though.

> Solicit the input of people who can give you insight into the problem, but avoid making <u>every</u> decision a group effort.

Although some of today's management styles strictly promote consensus or group decision-making, I believe it isn't always the most efficient and appropriate way to decide and implement every action. So, before we go any further, let's talk about the different methods and styles of decision making.

Decision Making Methods

Individual Decisions

This is when managers act alone. It's up to you to make the decision. You have enough information at your fingertips, and are familiar enough with your team's wants and needs to make the decision on your own.

Consultative Decisions

These are the types of decisions in which you feel as though you need some outside advice. So, with these decisions, it takes a little longer to gather the information you'll need and to ask others' opinions.

Group Decisions

This is when you involve your entire team in the decision making process. Sometimes you even back out of the way and let the team decide. This method gets greater team involvement and usually increases acceptance team buy-in. After all, why should they complain about a decision that was made by them?

What is key in identifying these methods of decision making is knowing when to use what method and be skilled enough in each method to make effective decisions.

Decision-Making Styles

Besides the different methods of decision making, managers also have diverse styles. Let's go over those:

The Democratic Style

In this style, majority rules—but, it does have its advantages. For instance, you get entire team participation, and a fairly quick decision. One big down side to this style is that there is no individual responsibility for the decision—none, except you as manager, that is.

The Autocratic Style

This style of decision making allows managers to maintain control of the process. Whether good or bad, it's your responsible. You're in charge! Although the decision- making process may be much faster, you may experience the total opposite when it comes to implementing the changes your decision requires. Those who had no ownership or input into making the decision may resent being left out of the process, and their resentment will be reflected in their lackluster follow-through with your particular plan of action.

Collective Participation

This is an invitation to participate. Managers don't call a mandatory meeting, but rather invite those who wish to attend and participate in the decision making. Those who participate are used more for their input and information than to make the final decision. Involvement is still the advantage, but time spent on the process could be your disadvantage.

Consensus

The leader gives up control of the decision altogether in this style of decision making. Only the group is involved in making the decision. The group, however, must realize that they will take responsibility for the outcome of that decision as well. There is usually great commitment to the outcome when decisions are made in this manner. Unfortunately, like collective participation, it is very time consuming and can be extremely labor intensive.

> If this is your preferred style, make sure that the time spent in the process isn't at the expense of achieving your sales quotas and customer service.

Choosing Your Options

Once you have determined your method of decision making and your style of decision making, it comes down to choosing between all your discovered alternatives and options. The last step, of course, is turning that choice into a plan of action and implementing that plan into your organization.

There are also many types of decisions managers face. Some are routine—the same circumstances—same proven course of action. Then there are the decisions that are more urgent, requiring the manager to think on his or her feet and make an on-the-spot choice. Those are obviously a lot more difficult. I don't know what's worse, having to make those decisions or having to wait for the results.

The most demanding of decisions are those involving strategic choices. These are choices in which managers must decide on aims and objectives and convert those into specific plans. That is one of the manager's most important tasks. If the only thing to be done was to sit around and think about one decision at a time, resolve that one and move on to the next—well, that wouldn't be so difficult. Those decisions are nice and orderly with plenty of time to gather and examine every option. No problem, right?

Also, what are the barriers to making strategic choices all the time? It just isn't how the business world works, especially not the sales industry.

> Managers must do all this while still being a visionary, making long-term decisions with the short term in mind, and handling sales teams with sensitivity and insight.

They need to know when to use what method and style of decision making. All this often keeps the manager on a tightrope between upper-management's demands and salespeople's desires.

Effective & Rewarding Tips for Better Decision Making

- This is the most important one of them all.

> DO NOT MAKE DECISIONS THAT ARE NOT YOURS TO MAKE!

- Avoid thinking in terms of right or wrong when involved in the decision making process. Instead, think of it as merely a choice between options.
- Know when to move quickly, or go more slowly in your decision making. If the decision can be easily reversed, it might be okay to make a snap decision. If it is a non-reversible decision, give yourself time to research your alternatives.
- Do your decision making on paper. Make notes. Keeps those notes in front of you. Review them and study them before making your decision.
- When you favor one alternative over another, be sure it is because of what is being offered—not who is offering it.
- Remember, not making a decision is really a decision not to act.
- As a manager, give yourself the right to be wrong!
- As part of your decision-making process, consider how this decision will be implemented—and by whom. That will give you an indication of who should be involved in the decision-making process along with you.
- Once the decision has been made, don't look back. That's the quickest way to lose your direction and forward momentum. Decide to have no regrets—you did the best you could at the time.
- Commit yourself to attaining positive results from your decision!

Barriers to Decision Making

There are also some barriers to decision making, and one of the biggest is fear.

Barrier #1: Fear

Fear comes from playing the "What if" game after making your decision. I suggest you play the "What if" game before making the decision. Give yourself a chance to examine all the what ifs.

- What if my decision costs too much or is too difficult to implement?
- What if I have very little buy-in from the team?_
- What if my decision doesn't get the positive result I planned on?
- What if my superiors think badly of me for choosing the wrong alternative?

Go ahead! Question yourself—but do it at a time where those questions can work **for** you rather than **against** you. If you play what if after you've made your decision—you'll just make yourself miserable.

> What ifs asked before the decision can give you a
> different perspective and perhaps change your choice.
> What ifs asked after can change your direction as well.
> From a progressive move toward your set plan, to a step
> backward in fear.

There are several traps that often plague the decision-making process. One is when you have failed to gather sufficient information to make your decision. Shooting from the hip might work on the rodeo circuit, but in business it can be a KILLER.

Barrier #2: Your Style is Collective Participation, and You Have a Group too Busy or too Lazy to Look at all the Alternatives

Instead, what is done is a solution based on one or two strong individual suggestions and the rest of the team just goes along. They get group fever; it's similar to cabin fever. Everybody gets tired, bored, restless and ready to bust out before the decision-making process has been concluded. So, they allow one or two, or even a handful of individuals to make the decision and the rest of the group simply agrees, assuming all other options were examined and investigated as much as necessary. It always amazed me when I was managing my companies how the most verbal complainers were those most unwilling to give their input in the decision-making process. Surprise! Surprise!

Barrier #3: Complaints

Speaking of complaints, they can be barriers to decision making, too. Instead of calling them complaints, I prefer to think of them as feedback. Much more positive, don't you think? I listen to the feedback and evaluate it, but, again, I do so before the decision has been made. That's the key. What's called feedback before the decision has been made is known as moaning and complaining afterwards.

Barrier #4: The Need for Dominance and Control

If you have one person or even a few who are more focused on controlling and dominating the situation than making the best decision for the entire team, you'll soon find that others will tire of the process and let the dominant players have their way. Then the decision doesn't reflect the needs of the many, but the desires of the verbal few.

I write down all the feedback received and distribute those comments to everyone for their review. It helps those who couldn't attend to look over all the feedback, perhaps giving them something to consider that they hadn't previously thought about. I also give the feedback to the outside sources we are using as consultants to the decision-making process. They can be invaluable, able to make suggestions from a vantage point of distance from the problem, which sometimes offers a clearer vision.

Barrier #5: Failure to Record the Results of Your Decisions and Evaluate their Outcomes

This is similar to a salesperson's win/loss review after meeting with a potential client. It is one of the most helpful tools for a manager during the decision-making process. Keeping records of your decisions will reveal to you just how similar many of your decisions are—and how predictable outcomes will be when you have proven results to review. Looking back on your methodology and style in the decision-making process can help you determine what methods and style will be best to use. Looking at the outcome of what happened with another similar decision might let you know what you'll be in for with this one.

As a manager, you are ultimately responsible for all the decisions made by you and your team. That can make you feel anxiety, but remember this:

All decisions come with risks and rewards.

Even those that didn't give you your desired results have rewards. As a manager, the worst thing to do is let fear make you indecisive.

What is often the cause of indecisiveness is that there is really no great, outstanding alternative that will make this problem go away. I'm sure you've heard the saying: "Caught between a rock and a hard place!"

> Many managers make decisions on a daily basis where there is no satisfactory conclusion—just one a little less disastrous than another.

Those are the decisions you'd like to give to the group, right?

Questions to Ask Yourself When Making Tough Decisions

1. What are my short- and long-term objectives?
2. Will the company make more money with this idea?
3. How much will we need to invest in marketing?
4. Will I need to recruit new people to implement my plan of action?
5. What happens if the marketplace changes and the idea falls flat?
6. What is the worst-case scenario? And, how would we deal with it should it occur?

By asking yourself these questions, you'll feel better prepared to address all the issues, both negative and positive, and be ready for the end results before making the decision.

A friend of mine once said, "Once you've determined you can live with the worst case scenario, you've got nowhere to go but up."

Are You Able to Make Decisions?

I've had you look at the different methods of decision making. We've examined the different styles, letting you determine which best suits your type of management. Now, let's look into a completely different area—ABILITY! Let's face it; some of us are just more able to make effective decisions.

For the most part, strong decision makers have had more experience.

From early childhood, I can remember being given the responsibility of decision-making, and encouraged to claim my own victories and suffer the consequences of my poor decisions. It wasn't always fun, but it certainly created that "I can do anything" attitude of a winner.

You know what, I honestly do believe I can do anything, which includes making great decisions. I may not make them the first time, but I'll eventually get to the right one. That is what I learned about decision making. Here's a story that illustrates my point. Harland was just a youngster when his father died, and perhaps that was part of the reason for his desperate need to succeed. He dropped out of school at 14-years old, his eagerness to be a success overriding his better judgment. He tried everything—farming, conductor of a streetcar, joined the Army, became a blacksmith, a railroad locomotive fireman, and even gave marriage a try. Being a good husband was a challenge to Harland, especially when his wife announced her pregnancy the day he was fired from his latest position. His wife couldn't stand the job-hunting, and one day Harland came home to an empty house, only to discover his wife had sold all their possessions and went back home to daddy. Then came our country's depression, and Harland tried his hand at still other opportunities: studying law, selling insurance, running a ferryboat then operating a filling station. You'd think Harland would have given up and accepted what most told him all his life—"Face it Harland—you're just a loser." Finally, at the age of 65, Harland made another decision that most thought to be another wild Harland Hair, but by this time Harland was angry. He was angry at life and people, and he turned that anger into something productive—determination to finally make the right decision. At 65 years old, Harland opened his first restaurant. Most of us know Harland as Colonel Sanders of Kentucky Fried Chicken. Do we question that Harland made the right decision? Well, at the end of his life it didn't matter much what people thought about his decision—he was an incredible success.

If at first you don't make the right decision, back up, sharpen your decision- making abilities, dig your heals in, and jump back into the fire!

It took a long time for Colonel Sanders to overcome that first poor decision, and some of us experience the same setbacks.

It's never a poor decision that holds people back, it's their failure to overcome that keeps most people from success.

As you learn the process of becoming a great decision maker, you will soon see the difference between the levels of ability from one decision maker to another. Sometimes the only thing that separates excellent decision-makers from the average is their ability to keep on trying!

There are two categories of decision makers; 1) Those who make decisions intuitively; and, 2) Those who make decisions logically. The intuitive decision makers base their decisions on creativity and spontaneity. While the logical decision makers base their choices on rational facts and careful judgment. There is no right or wrong way, just a tendency to do more of one than another. Again, I would stress to you the importance of balance. Keeping that balance enables you to be a much more effective and powerful decision-maker whose outcomes are usually on the positive side. Let's take a closer look at these two categories of decision makers and you can determine which one best fits your style of management.

Intuitive Decision Maker

If you are in this category of decision-maker, you tend to play your hunches. You lean more toward emotions than logic when making your decisions, and you are more sensitive to others' insights and responses to your decisions. The best attributes you have are your creativity, imagination and your willingness to hear other viewpoints.

Logical Decision Maker

You are more of an analytical type of decision-maker. You use knowledge, skills and experience to determine what choice is best for you and your team. You logically analyze every alternative before making your choice in order to understand the bigger picture.

Looking at these two categories, I'm sure some of you are thinking, "No question, Omar, I'd rather be the logical decision maker." Not so fast! Think about it.

> Most people, including your customers, make decisions emotionally and then justify those decisions logically.

If you don't understand their style of decision-making, it could be difficult to come to a successful close. One way is really no better than another! It's the combination, the flexibility to interchange these methods, styles and categories that create the best decision makers.

One of the most influential components to the decision-making process is how your corporate culture affects your decisions. When examining how your company could be affecting your decisions, ask the following questions:

1. Are new ideas welcomed or dismissed by your company?
2. Is your company customer-driven, or is their approach to problem solving more internal?
3. Does your company focus on the problem or the opportunity those problems create?
4. Are your company's most valued traits motivation and innovation, or stability and experience?
5. Does your company seek to align corporate and individual objectives, or do they put the good of the company before the success of the individual?
6. Are the policies and philosophies of your company experiencing constant growth and evolution, or is change almost unheard of in your corporate mindset?

Although the questions I just asked you to consider are rather polarized—one extreme or the other—your company might be more toward middle ground on some of those issues. You might be wondering, "Omar, what does company culture have to do with my decision-making abilities, anyway?" Well, I'll tell you; if new ideas are welcomed, you and your team feel safe about being innovative in your suggestions and decisions. It's really based on safety issues. How safe do you feel to be a decision maker within your organization?

How much can you trust yourself and others to make decisions that will not compromise your position? That trust is critical in some methods of decision-making, but your company's culture might be fighting you on this one.

> Your feelings will trickle down to your people. If you are unsure, they too will be unsure and indecisive. If you hesitate to accept change—so will they. If you fear making important decisions and constantly belabor them—so will your team.

Not every decision is made in blood or carved in stone. Knowing this may help you to go against your company culture once in a while without feeling like you are balancing on a tightrope over Niagara Falls.

Types of Decisions

Irreversible
These are decisions that, no matter how bad, cannot be unmade. Like selling the company or signing an agreement. The great thing about irreversible decisions are that they definitely do not make up the majority of your decisions.

Reversible
These will be much more comfortable for you to make. They can be completely changed before, during or after the decision-making process.

Experimental
These are the types of decisions that are not final until the first results appear.

Trial and Error
These are the changes that will occur depending on what happens as a result of your decision.

Made in Stages
After you make the initial decision, further, smaller decisions will follow at each stage of your action plan.

Cautious
These are the type of flexible decisions that allow for problems or challenges that may occur later.

Conditional
This is the either/or decision. It's made with the ability to keep your options open.

Delayed
This is a decision you put on hold until the time is right.

I'm giving you all these because different decisions require different approaches. Isn't it time for you to make a forecast for your future that you're going to be a winning decision-maker? You can! Based on the experience you already have and the leadership skills you'll learn in this book, you can create a positive future.

What do you need to do?

1. Assume success is for you!
2. Be fearless in your decision-making.
3. Surround yourself with professionals who can help you make effective decisions.
4. Provide the necessary education and training for your team and yourself to keep you on the pulse of the industry.
5. Solicit the ideas and insights of your team.

Then take MASSIVE action! **So What's MASSIVE Action?**

M = **MASTER** the skills needed to lead your people to greater heights of success.

A = Maintain the **ATTITUDE** of a winner and teach your people to do the same.

S = **SERVE** your salespeople; they are your customers.

S = **SUPPORT** and trust their decisions.

I = Be **INNOVATIVE** with your team, allowing them the freedom to create their own challenges and opportunities.

V = Be a **VISIONARY** leader. Help your people to see the bigger picture.

E = Show love and **ENTHUSIASM** for your work.

Before you know it, your energy will begin to spread to your entire sales team, and your team will become known for its exceptional decision-making skills.

Working Through the Process--Chapter Six

❖ What are the positives and negatives of your decision-making capabilities?

Positives	Negatives

❖ What has been one of the best decisions of your management career? Why?

_____

_____

_____

❖ Using the above example, explain your decision-making process.

Options Considered:

_____

_____

Plan of Action:

_____

_____

Implementation of Plan:

_____

_____

Adjustments:

_____

_____

Measurement of Success:

_____

_____

Outcome of Similar Decisions:

_____

_____

❖ Using the previous decision, what were its possible risks and rewards?

Risks:

_____

_____

Rewards:

_____

_____

❖ List at least five decisions you've made over the past 12 months. Have those decisions tended to be more intuitive or logical? What were the results of those decisions?

Decision	Intuitive/Logical	Results
_____	_____	_____
_____	_____	_____
_____	_____	_____
_____	_____	_____
_____	_____	_____

❖ How has your decision-making style been influenced by your corporate culture?

_____

_____

❖ How have you taken MASSIVE action in your decision-making?

M   =   MASTERED Management Skills

_____

A   =   Adopted the ATTITUDE of a Winner

_____

S   =   SERVED your people

_____

S   =   SUPPORTED your people

_____

I   =   Encouraged INNOVATIVE thinking

_____

V   =   Been a VISIONARY leader

_____

E   =   Maintained an ENTHUSIASM for selling

_____

CHAPTER SEVEN

Aim High--Setting Success Goals vs. Setting Sales Goals

"Goals give purpose. Purpose give faith. Faith gives courage. Courage gives enthusiasm. Enthusiasm gives energy. Energy give life. Life lifts you over the bar."

Bob Richards (Pole Vaulter)

Chapter Highlights:

▶ Why Write Down Your Goals?
▶ Setting Goals or Breaking Resolutions?
▶ From Vague Wants to Vivid Goals
▶ Picture Your Passions
▶ Discovering Your Dreams
▶ Learning the Simple Three-Part Goal System
▶ Experiencing the Moment of Truth

I'm sure by now in your careers, many of you have been through goal-setting workshops or seminars that supposedly taught you and encouraged you to set goals. Don't tell me—I suspect your comments when you first turned to this chapter on goal setting went something like this: "Okay, I'll just skip this chapter and move on to the next." Or perhaps you were thinking, "I've heard this stuff a hundred times, and I just don't feel the necessity to set goals."

Let me ask you a question—Do you expect your salespeople to set and meet, or even exceed, their goals?

> If you're going to be the teacher, you must first become the student. Learn to set and meet your own goals before attempting to help your salespeople with goal-setting principles.

I feel quite comfortable in issuing this challenge: when you become a goal-oriented leader, you will achieve greater heights of success than you ever thought possible. And, when your success skyrockets, your salespeople will get the idea that there just might be something to this goal setting stuff after all. Next thing you know, your people will be setting and achieving their goals as well.

I suspect that I've got my work cut out for me, but I'm up for the challenge. I have a goal here myself: to help you, your family, and your sales force achieve the maximum from this book. I usually achieve what I set out to—so I'm not about to give up graciously and let you off the hook.

Who Needs to Write Down Goals? I Know What I Want!

First, I'll talk to those of you who do not set goals. There are probably some good reasons why you don't. You have accomplished great things without them, so you don't need them, right? You know what you want and are constantly striving toward that end. Or, you tried setting goals in the past but never achieved success, so you decided it was much less frustrating to just forget about goal setting. I know those excuses well because I have used every one of them a time or two myself.

All those are reasonable reasons not to set goals, but did you know that the top performers in every field are people who set specific goals and develop a plan of action to achieve those goals?

> Let me ask you another question—if you have done so well without setting goals, can you imagine what a powerhouse you'd be with goals put into place? WOW! You'd be unbeatable!

Are You Setting Goals or Breaking Resolutions?

For most of you who don't set goals, you may not be familiar with the difference between a few important terms that are commonly confused with goals.

For example, when you ask some managers if they set goals, they say, "Oh yes, Omar, once a year I look back over what I accomplished the year before and congratulate myself. Then I look at what I want for this year and get to work. Yep, I set goals."

I beg to differ with you, but those aren't goals—they're resolutions. And, resolutions are made to be broken.

> Most of the time resolutions set on January 1st are broken before the next weekend rolls around.

If you think goal setting is about making a bold statement once a year, it's not. Resolutions rarely call for the development of a plan of action to help you achieve. Instead, they have you waiting an entire year to celebrate your success or discover where you went wrong. Resolutions put you on track all right—on track for failure, disappointments or disillusionments.

Can you see the differences between resolutions and goals? Resolutions are once a year, with no plan, no rewards for your successes and no consequences for your setbacks. Because of this, there is no commitment to even that one statement on New Year's Eve night. Resolutions are made to be broken and laughed about the following year.

On the other hand, goals are usually set once a month rather than once a year. They are written down with an expected time frame for achievement and specific steps that will constantly move you toward your goals. That's your plan of action. Goals are reviewed at least once a week, and evaluated bi-monthly to keep you on track. They are followed up with a daily plan of attack—which I refer to as your "to do" list. See the difference? Of course, you may be setting long-term goals that have different time frames and longer periods between rewards and consequences, but for the most part short-term goals work in this way.

Turning Vague Wants Into Vivid Goals

Now let me speak to those of you who say, "Omar, I know what I want. I just keep working hard until I achieve it, then I move on to the next thing." For those of you who think this way, you have your wants mixed up with your goals. Everybody wants, don't they? I remember when my mentor, Mr. Murphy, told me to set a goal to become a millionaire. I wanted to become a millionaire. Is there anyone who wouldn't? The difference is, I had a mentor who asked me serious questions and kept me accountable. I set out a plan to achieve my want. I studied, read, listened to tapes of great salespeople, and attended seminars to get my vision clear about what I wanted to set as my goal. Then I set a time frame on my goal to become a millionaire. I said, "I will be a millionaire by the time I'm 31." Notice the difference in wording. It was no longer "I want" but "I will." I didn't stop there. Most of all, I was willing to do whatever it took to achieve that goal. I trained my voice for 8 hours a day. I worked out in the gym until my muscles cramped up. I studied sales from almost every great speaker and trainer in the world. I was always on the lookout to meet highly successful people who were already at the place I saw myself going. When given the opportunity, I questioned them to soak up every bit of knowledge and insight they could give.

Picture Your Passion

The best thing I did was pictured myself as a millionaire when I was only making $147 dollars a month as a young, inexperienced salesperson. I was relentless, and I had a burning passion for success. Now that's commitment to a goal. See the difference? Goals are your wants, backed up by incredible emotion, a burning passion and belief that you will achieve, and an image of yourself as one who is already there.

Sports figures use this "picturing" technique too. Michael Jordan says this about picturing his goal at the free-throw line: "If I had stood at the free-throw line and thought about 10 million people watching me on the other side of the camera lens, I couldn't have made anything. So I mentally tried to put myself in a familiar place. I thought about all those times I shot free throws in practice and went through the same motion, the same technique that I had used thousands of time. You forget about the outcome. You know you are doing the right things. So you relax and perform." Obviously, Michael is very comfortable with picturing his success. However, for most people, picturing and attaining goals takes a lot of concentration and hard work.

Goals take a lot of energy, so I consider them <u>energized wants</u>. You might say: goals are wants that pack a wallop! There are really three simple questions to ask yourself when determining your goals. Here they are:

1. **Where am I now?**
    Once you have a clear picture of where you are, then it's time you understand a few things about a "WANT" or desire to be somewhere

different. Keep in mind; if you always want to be where you are now, then there is no need for goals, for changes in your life. Just keep on doing today what you did yesterday, and all your days will be alike, right? Well, not exactly. Think about it. What if you handled yourself today just like you did 20 years ago? What would your career be like? Do you think you'd still be able to be the type of person you are today? Probably not. Now, you more efficiently manage your people through the use of high tech equipment and communications. So, you can't ever rest on your laurels, because that's exactly the time you'll begin to roll backwards.

Ask yourself these questions when you are determining where you are now.
- Do you truly believe you can achieve your goals?
- Are you willing to pay the price—to do what it takes to accomplish your goals?
- Can you repeat the success to ensure ongoing achievement in all areas of your professional life, your personal life, your spiritual life and your family life?

2.   Now, what got you where you are today?
If you really like where you are, what did you do right to get there? Also, think about where you could have been if you had set a few more goals along the way. If you don't like the place you are at right now, then where is it you want to be? Who do you want to become? How do you plan to become that person? That leads us to the next point.

3.   Where do you want to go?
For some of us, determining our dreams and aspirations and setting goals to achieve them is a very difficult task. Let me give you some pointers.

> Avoid adopting others' dreams as your own. They won't fit, and you won't feel comfortable with your accomplishments even if you do achieve goals that aren't yours.

Why? Because it really wasn't your dream—it was somebody else's. It's okay to be a little selfish when you discover your dreams and set your goals.

Catch the Goal Fever

Once you get goal setting down, you'll be surprised at how contagious it can be to your salespeople. Let me share with you a story: I taught goal setting to a friend of mine who wanted to lose weight. She admits now that she was motivated by what she heard, but she just didn't do what I had taught her. Instead, she talked to others about my goal setting process. First she talked to her husband, who adopted my principles for himself and lost 65 pounds in four months. Then she talked to her partner, who set her goal to lose 15 pounds, wrote down her reward and consequence for the goal, and she too achieved her goal. After about six people had adopted my principles and achieved their goals, she was finally convinced there could be something to my goal-setting principles. Now she is on a healthy eating and exercise plan, she has lost 22 pounds, and she has a vision of herself as already being a fit, attractive woman.

Discover Your Dreams

What about you? Do you believe you can achieve? If so, what is it you want? First discover your dreams—the ones about which you are really passionate. Then picture yourself as if you have already attained success. One of my dreams was to become a millionaire, so after I prepared for my achievement, I began convincing myself through a clear vision of how I would look and act as a millionaire.

I bought an Armani suit. When I put that suit on and looked in the mirror, I said, "This is me!" It felt comfortable and right. Then I invested in a Mercedes. Now, it wasn't a new Mercedes, I couldn't afford that yet. It was older but in great shape, and I purchased it at a very reasonable price. What was I doing with my picturing technique? I was working to create the image of myself within that vision.

Sharing the Vision

I shared my goals with those I trusted and loved. The more people I told, the more accountable I became. I knew it would take a lot of hard work, so I was sure to keep myself on track by keeping my daily "to do" list and checking off my accomplishments. Each day I was one day closer to becoming a millionaire. If I experienced setbacks, and I did, I refused to give up. There was no way out but admitting to failure, and I wasn't about to do that. So, when I had a setback in one area, I backtracked to where I went off course and then headed in another direction.

Isn't that what you do when you're on a journey? Think of goal setting as your journey to success. If you miss a turn and get headed in the wrong direction, you just backtrack a little bit until you find your way again. You may have to refer to your map—just like I review my goals all the time, but it keeps me headed in the right direction.

Eliminating the Inconsistencies

I'd like to speak to those of you who set goals periodically, but are fairly inconsistent, and you feel more like you are just having a "hot" streak when you achieve your goals. Here's what I would ask you? First of all, how passionate were you about achieving the goal? If you didn't have the passion to achieve it, the goal may have really been just a casual or vague want.

As I said before, setting and achieving goals are hard work. They require things of us that we wouldn't normally do if that goal weren't in place to motivate us. Are you willing to do what it takes to be successful? What does that mean to you as a manager? Ask yourself:

- Will I invest the time and money in myself to learn how to be a GREAT leader?
- Will I invest the time and money to provide training for my people? If it requires taking a chance and stepping out on a limb for my people— am I committed to that goal?
- When helping my people set and achieve their individual and team goals, can I step out of the way and let them forge their own path to success?
- Am I able to stand up to those traditional thinkers, the "sacred cows" and fight for my team to create expanded opportunities for my people?
- Do I have a plan that will recognize and reward their success? Do I have a plan that will catch temporary setbacks before they become a total block to accomplishing the goal?

The only way you can be consistently successful is to set specific goals and develop definite action plans to achieve those goals. It can't be a one-year resolution or a vague want. No!

Aim high—be deliberate and vivid in your goal statements and the steps you'll take to achieve those goals. That's how you'll repeat your successes, year after year, month after month, week after week, day after day.

Everybody wants to belong to a winning team. If you can sustain or create goal after goal, getting into the habit of happy, fulfilling achievement, you won't have trouble recruiting people or keeping the top producers you have developed. The key is that you must, once again, teach by example. Be a goal setter yourself.

Now that you have asked yourself those three important goal questions, how about doing the same with your salespeople. Is your sales team on a success course with their goals? How do your salespeople perceive themselves? As their leader and coach, you play a very important part in their ability to achieve.

What pictures of success are you creating with your words to your salespeople?
After a sales meeting with your people, ask yourself...

Yes No
❏   ❏   1. How do my salespeople leave me?
❏   ❏   2. Do they feel good about themselves?
❏   ❏   3. Are they eager to try out some suggested strategies?
❏   ❏   4. Are they leaving my office with their heads down, feeling defeated?
❏   ❏   5. Do they speak with confidence and assurance?
❏   ❏   6. Whenever they are around me do they hesitate to speak up and offer their opinion?
❏   ❏   7. Do they walk with purpose?
❏   ❏   8. Do they have good health and attendance?
❏   ❏   9 Do they meet their quotas and deadlines and still have energy to spare?
❏   ❏   10. Do they envision disaster striking the next quarter and all their work being for nothing?

Now total your positives and negatives. If you are seeing a lot of the negative instead of the positive pictures, look at the way you manage your people. I don't want you to feel totally responsible for their every mood swing and unproductive day, but if you can do something about the negatives—let's figure out what that something could be and then go for it!

First of all, I challenge you to commit to your salespeople with my commitment form, and see your salespeople the way you want them to become. Even those slugs—don't let them go just yet!

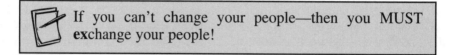

> If you can't change your people—then you MUST **ex**change your people!

In simple terms—it may be necessary for you to let some salespeople go and reorganize your team. Give the ones who stay with you a higher aim than what they had yesterday. Encourage them to dream. Speak to them in terms of what they are doing right. Start teaching my simple three-part goals system. What? You haven't learned it yet? Well, here goes--very easy.

STEP #1 – Identify Three Dreams

Make one dream take place in your professional career life—one in your personal life—one in your family life. Now write specific goal statements from these dreams. Statements that reflect beliefs as if you are already there. Here's an example of a goal statement: "I am physically fit, weighing 20 pounds less and fitting into a size 10, as I review this goal 60 days from now." Or, if it's for one of your salespeople, it could go something like this: "I have landed that new account and am now working toward an agreement with the three referrals they gave me as I look back over this goal on July 15th."

STEP #2 – Write Achievement Steps to Your Goals

Write at least three steps for each goal. Then record the way you will reward yourself and the consequences you will suffer if you achieve or do not achieve your goal. Make sure that your rewards and consequences are strong enough to make you passionate about achievement. Make your reward something you would never treat yourself to, unless you could cover its cost or justify the reward because you achieved great success. Make the consequences so unbearable that it is inconceivable for you to fail. These are key to my goal-setting principles.

Let me give you some examples. If you set a goal to double your business and you have the activities written down that you'll have to do to make that happen, now what will be your reward or consequence? Will your reward be a new home?—A trip to Europe?—That new boat you've been dreaming about? Will your consequence be if you should not achieve your dream that you send your competitor to Europe for doing all the things you should have been doing? Or, will your consequence be that you buy the boat and keep it stored until you achieve your goal? You see how strong your consequences must be?

Another thing to realize about rewards and consequences is that they need to be frequent enough to create urgency. In other words, if this goal will take two years to accomplish, you've got to reward yourself along the way. Or, set up consequences to check your progress. If not, you will be unable to sustain your higher level of performance.

STEP #3 = TAKE MASSIVE ACTION

Wouldn't it be a shame to have taken all this time to write down your goals, only to bury them somewhere in your desk never to be looked at again? Promise me you won't do that.

Tips to Sustain Your Success Momentum

- Keep goals in a prominent place and review them frequently.
- Keep a "to do" list in your daily planner.
- Be a risk-taker. Set a high and low range to your goals. Reaching the peak would be incredible, but missing the low would be unthinkable.
- Never stop setting goals. Keep a goals' journal—a journal of your success.
- Make up your mind to be more than a survivor in this business—be a peak performer—a super achiever!

Maintain a NO FEAR Goal Setting Policy

Make sure you have NO FEAR of negative judgment for aiming too high and missing the mark. Have NO FEAR of envy or isolation when you reach high goals and your co-workers don't. Let your salespeople know there is NO FEAR of having the rewards for high achievement by raised quotas and unreasonable expectations.

Refuse to accept the standard excuses of why your salespeople didn't achieve their set goals. If it's difficult for you, you'll be able to empathize with their struggles, but not too much. Don't give them an easy way out. Let me prepare you for some of the common excuses you could receive from your salespeople. You'll recognize them; in fact, you've probably used some of them.

- I couldn't write down my goals—I just didn't have the time.
- I already know what I want—there was no need to write down my goals.
- I was afraid if I wrote them down and didn't achieve them I'd feel like a failure.
- I had so many goals I couldn't keep track of them all. Writing them down didn't make any difference.

Indifference Is A Dream Killer

One of the biggest killers of motivation to achieve is indifference. Indifference actually creates false contentment. You tell yourself you "CAN'T" then convince yourself you "DON'T WANT" to anyway. Why not tell yourself you "CAN" then change your "WANTS" into your "REALITY"?

Life is not meant to be a casual, accidental experience. Be deliberate about your success. Be passionately on fire for selling success with your team and yourself. The lull of indifference is a success distracter. At the crossroads of choice, make the right choice a habit. Help your salespeople choose to work instead of taking that two-hour lunch with the gang. Show your people the importance of using those 20 minutes before the sales meeting to do paperwork instead of play solitaire on the computer. Show them the value of choosing to follow-up one more time with the "NO" customer. Choose the positive possibilities of persistence.

The key is to make a plan that will allow you to determine clear choices before you reach that moment of truth. For example, don't make a goal to cut all sweets out of your eating program and then stock up on candy bars when you're grocery shopping. Don't commit to turning around your quarterly figures then plan a week's vacation that will eat up your selling time. Don't sabotage your goals—make a commitment to succeed and your salespeople will follow close behind!

The Moment of Truth

You will reach, sometime during the time frame you have allowed yourself to achieve your goal, a time I call the moment of truth. At this moment, your temptation to slide back into old patterns and behaviors that brought you mediocre achievements will be equally as strong as your commitment to achieve your goal. You will be better prepared to continue an upward momentum at that moment of truth and make a good choice that will lead you to your goal if you have strengthened your resolve along the way by counting your small victories.

For this reason, I encourage you to keep a notebook, or even a log in your computer, of all the goals you have achieved. Review it frequently! Relive your success. Talk about them with your significant other, your co-workers, your family and friends. Those who love you will encourage you. They may be what makes the difference at that moment of truth.

Not that one poor choice is going to ruin your entire chance to achieve your goal. Look at it as a temporary setback and move on. Pretty soon, your choices at these moments of truth will be as simple as a question of:

Will it take me toward my goal or away from my goal?

The choices you make will be automatic, and your path to success will no longer be paved with good intentions—but, rather, with outstanding achievements.

Working Through the Process--Chapter Seven

❖ Where are you now in your management career?

_____

_____

❖ What changes would you like to see this year in your management methods and style?

_____

_____

❖ Are you willing to do what it takes to become a GREAT manager?

Yes_____   No _____   Depends_____

❖ List three of your top career goals and five steps to achieving those goals.

Goal: _____

Step #1 _____

Step #2 _____

Step #3 _____

Step #4 _____

Step #5 _____

Goal: _____

Step #1 _____

Step #2 _____

Step #3 _____

Step #4 _____

Step #5 _____

Goal: _____

Step #1 _____

Step #2 _____

Step #3 _____

Step #4 _____

Step #5 _____

❖ Who do you plan to communicate your goals to? How will they help to hold you accountable?

_____

_____

❖ What could hinder or prohibit your achievement of these goals?

_____

_____

❖ Maintain a NO FEAR goal setting and maintenance program.

   1. NO FEAR of _____ _____ for setting your goals to high.

   2. NO FEAR of _____ and _____ when you reach high goals.

   3. NO FEAR of _____ for not reaching a high goal.

   4. NO FEAR of being given _____ _____, raised _____, or more difficult _____ when you successfully achieve your goals.

❖ What will the achievement of these goals mean to you and your sales team?

_____

_____

_____

❖ How will you...
   Be rewarded?

_____

   Celebrate your success?

_____

   Encourage your salespeople to do the same?

_____

❖ What will be the consequences for not following your commitment to achieving your goals?

_____

_____

CHAPTER EIGHT
Training for Today's Marketplace

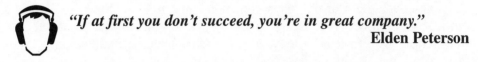

"If at first you don't succeed, you're in great company."
Elden Peterson

Chapter Highlights:

▶ Perceived Dangers of Training
▶ Win/Loss Review
▶ The Training Triangle
▶ The Four Levels of Training
▶ The 12 Tactics & Strategies for Selling Success
▶ Who Needs Training?
▶ Training Models
▶ Seven Winning Character Traits of a Great Manager

Instead of focusing on all the positives of training, some managers look at the dangers of investing in training in today's market. To put your mind at rest, let's examine ways to anticipate and overcome the dangers. Then we can put them aside and focus on all the positives you'll receive through effective training by the experts.

What are the perceived dangers of investing in training? For one, job longevity has been declining in recent years, and the movement makes management feel insecure about investing in training for their new recruits only to have them take all that knowledge to another company. Competitors benefit while someone else picks up the tab for training. Let me challenge you to see things in a different light. Instead of seeing danger in training, I'd like you to look at it through the eyes of a leader. When you do, you'll realize that offering excellent training will literally keep your people with you and your company.

 I believe that top producers are developed, not born. If that is true, then as a manager, you have the opportunity to mold your new recruits through exceptional training.

You can coach them in the ways your company prefers. Since an important part of the selling process is knowing your company and its products and services, your salespeople won't want to leave a great learning environment only to start the process all over again. Make their career a challenging and rewarding experience with your company, and you'll keep your top salespeople and develop your newcomers to become their best.

Another perceived danger is that your people will not implement the new skills that you've provided through training. Consequently, their sales ratios will not be reflective of your training investment, and they could actually make your decision to train look bad to your superiors.

One way to overcome and change your views about this perceived danger is to make sure your program has regularly scheduled follow-up training, peer coaching and evaluation.

Your salespeople may have many excuses for not implementing the new skills they have learned, but I have discovered that it often boils down to ONE thing—they don't want to increase their performance **bad enough**.

The last words "bad enough" are key to that last statement. Some of your salespeople may want to improve their performance, but they just don't want to improve "bad enough" to do what it takes to become their best. They aren't willing to pay the price—to make the sacrifices necessary to achieve greater success. To justify their behavior, some will think up other reasons why they haven't implemented those new strategies and skills learned at their last training.

Then I have found that many people actually believe they are implementing the new skills, but for some strange reason the things they learned just aren't working. In reality, they may have been going through the motions but didn't believe the newly learned skills would actually do what their trainer promised. Before long, they dropped the new skill and returned to their old habits. Or, they have implemented a version of the new skills but are performing them inaccurately or inadequately, so their results are far below what was expected.

By investing in training with strong follow-up programs and continued coaching, you'll be able to help develop your people to their highest potential. How? The following are just a few suggestions:

- Set up self-evaluation programs and regular reviews.
- Ask that your people fill out activity sheets with listed outcomes.
- Review those activity sheets frequently, and discuss with your people how they could improve their areas of concern.
- Praise them for the activities they are currently implementing and allow them to share their accomplishments with other team members during your sales meetings.

Another effective management tool is a Win/Loss Review Form. In case you've never used this method of evaluation, they are forms that are filled out by the salesperson after making a sales call. Whether that particular call resulted in a positive close (a win) or a temporary setback (a loss), the form encourages your people to keep a record of their performance. Then, when they enter into negotiations or a presentation that is similar to one they have experienced in the past, they will be able to see what worked and what didn't. Having successes recorded makes it possible to duplicate them because the successes act as reminders of what they did right. They also let your people see patterns of behavior that need to change. The following two pages offer a sample Win/Loss Review Form:

WIN/LOSS REVIEW

GENERAL INFORMATION

Sales Representative:_____   **Date:**_____
Division/Group:_____
Customer Name(s):_____
Title:_____

DATES:
Won   Lost   Date Confirmed:_____
Date of First Contact (this opportunity):_____
Date of Last Face-to-Face Contact:_____

COMPETITION:
Top Three Competitors
Competitor #1:_____
Customer Perceived Strengths:
_____
_____

Customer Perceived Weaknesses:
_____
_____

Competitor's Strategies:
_____
_____

Competitor #2:_____
Customer Perceived Strengths:
_____
_____

Customer Perceived Weaknesses:
_____
_____

Competitor's Strategies:
_____
_____

Competitor #3:_____
Customer Perceived Strengths:
_____
_____

Customer Perceived Weaknesses:
_____
_____

Competitor'sStrategies:
_____
_____

YOUR BUSINESS:
Strengths:
_____
_____

Weaknesses:
_____
_____

What Customer Needs Were Identified?
_____
_____

What Were Barriers to Winning the Account?
_____
_____

What Would You Do Differently?
_____
_____

If you invest in an expert to train your people, and practice sound coaching and proper follow-up, your returns will far exceed your superior's expectations. However, it's not all your responsibility; it's a mutually vested venture. If your salespeople don't want to invest their time to learn, your investment won't get maximum returns.

> Your salespeople need to have an **attitude for learning**, the **enthusiasm to succeed** and the **motivation to continue** the work to improve.

Let me illustrate for you how I have worked with salespeople and managers to provide the necessary tools to achieve greatness.

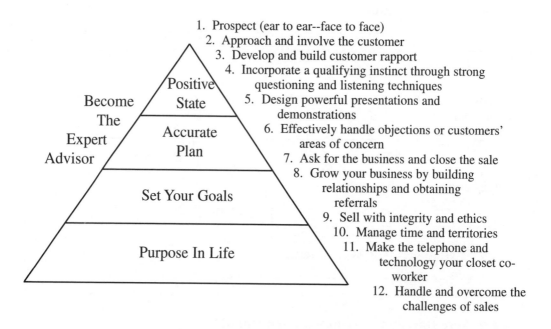

1. Prospect (ear to ear--face to face)
2. Approach and involve the customer
3. Develop and build customer rapport
4. Incorporate a qualifying instinct through strong questioning and listening techniques
5. Design powerful presentations and demonstrations
6. Effectively handle objections or customers' areas of concern
7. Ask for the business and close the sale
8. Grow your business by building relationships and obtaining referrals
9. Sell with integrity and ethics
10. Manage time and territories
11. Make the telephone and technology your closet co-worker
12. Handle and overcome the challenges of sales

Become The Expert Advisor — Positive State — Accurate Plan — Set Your Goals — Purpose In Life

I call it the TRAINING TRIANGLE. At the top of this triangle are your top producers who have those three things I just spoke of—a learning **attitude**, the **enthusiasm** to succeed, and the **motivation** to continue their work to improve. At the base of my TRAINING TRIANGLE is a sound foundation of training. It is much like Maslow's pyramid, only there are four levels of training.

Level #1:   Trainer and manager help salespeople and support staff to identify their PURPOSE for training. What do they want to achieve? What are their dreams?

Level #2:   The trainer and coach help their people to SET GOALS to achieve their stated PURPOSE in Level #1. At Level #2, people are able to see exactly what it will take to achieve their dreams. Goals are not to be taken lightly. If it is difficult for your people to set GOALS at this level, then you need to return to Level #1 and discover a stronger purpose, a more compelling reason for them to achieve.

Level #3:   Once the goals have been set to include appropriate time frames, progressive reviews and effective evaluations, the trainer and coach help their people establish an ACCURATE PLAN OF ACTION. This plan includes their daily activities your people will need to do in order to consistently achieve those goals and reach their dreams. Unfortunately, here's where the training can fall apart. Developing a specific plan for your people requires a good bit of coaching from you, as manager.

Even exceptional trainers do not know your people like you know your people. That's what divides a manager from a leader—their ability to assist salespeople in establishing a workable, challenging PLAN OF ACTION to help them implement their new skills and strategies.

Level #4:   This top level relates to your salespeople's state of mind. In order to help them become their best, to use the training you provide to its highest advantage, managers must work with each individual salesperson's belief system. Does this particular salesperson positively KNOW that the achievement of his or her dreams is a reality? If not, lead them through baby steps first and work up to the bigger achievements. Provide beginning training with specific follow-up and work up to the advanced skills when they clearly have the others in place and are ready to move forward.   Notice how the word "listen" kept cropping up?

Most of all, as coach, **listen** and encourage, **listen** and advise, **listen** and trust.

Listening is crucial in training and coaching your people to believe they can achieve.

To the left of the Training Triangle, I teach managers to instruct their people to become the expert advisor. This means their people will need to become masters at presenting the company's products and services. Today's method of sales is consultative, added value selling, and to consult with others the salesperson must become the master. To insure great success, at the right of the Training Triangle I've put together Twelve Tactics and Strategies for Selling Success. These are the selling components your people must know to succeed in the new millennium marketplace. And, guess whose job it is to make sure these skills are introduced and perfected—the manager's.

Twelve Tactics and Strategies for Selling Success

1. Prospect (ear to ear—face to face)
2. Approach and involve the customer
3. Develop and build customer rapport
4. Incorporate a qualifying instinct through strong questioning and listening techniques
5. Design powerful presentations and demonstrations
6. Effectively handle objections or customers' areas of concern
7. Ask for the business and close the sale
8. Grow your business by building relationships and obtaining referrals
9. Sell with integrity and ethics
10. Manage time and territories
11. Make the telephone and technology your closest co-worker
12. Handle and overcome the challenges of sales

Attaining the highest level and the best results from training means effectively implementing all twelve tactics and strategies.

There are things you can be doing as a manager to make sure your people are suited to your company, product, industry, management style and customer base—things to do before investing costly training dollars. Commit yourself to becoming a people developer and get the budget and support of upper-management decision makers.

Here's My Seven Point Checklist

- ✔ Make a training schedule.
- ✔ Do an analysis of program investment and estimated returns.
- ✔ Present your people's needs and requirements to your company's decision makers. Sell the value of a comprehensive training program.
- ✔ Compare the objectives of your sales team with company objectives. Align them. What do you want? What do your salespeople need? How can you satisfy their needs and still get what you want? What training is best suited to ensure you and your salespeople's success?
- ✔ Lay out a complete program. Don't look at training as a piecemeal endeavor. Have a long-range vision for you and your team's success.
- ✔ View training as a living, breathing evolution of skills that grow and change with the needs of the team and each of its members.
- ✔ Make sure the trainer you choose has a clear vision of your company and team's objectives.

Who Needs Training?

Great managers and leaders recognize the fact that every new salesperson needs training, but who else should be trained? What about your telemarketers? What about your marketing support representatives? Then, of course, there are your veteran salespeople. They'll need to be challenged with innovative training and instruction that reinforces the fundamentals. Lastly, but probably most important, what about you as the sales manager?

If you have been promoted up through the ranks of salespeople, you probably began your career as an eager salesperson, then progressed to top producer in your company, and now you've finally moved into management. Well, while the other promotions were a natural progression of your already learned skills, management is a whole different ball game, isn't it? It requires an entirely different set of skills; for most of you, it's a new SELL. Now your <u>product</u> is <u>people development</u> and your <u>customers</u> are your <u>salespeople</u>.

Because of this, you're starting all over again—and you'll need special management training in how to help your people become their best. This is why I feel privileged that many of you have invested in this book—because you've recognized the need for long-term, continuous sales and sales management training. Now that we've identified who needs training, let's look at what type of training each of these categories require.

<u>New Salespeople or New Employees—What They'll Need to Know</u>
1.   Basic selling skills
2.   Company information and background
3.   What is expected of them administratively—what paperwork do they need to complete and what are the processing requirements of that paperwork?
4.   Your company's product line and the services you provide
5.   How you recommend demonstrating and presenting your products and services
6.   How to avoid team disputes—if your team has territories and specified accounts, your new people will need to know that information as well
7.   The marketplace and industry—even if they've sold before, they may have dealt with an entirely different product or service

<u>Veteran Salespeople</u>
1.   Veterans need to be challenged by learning advanced selling strategies.
2.   Although they may be familiar with their favorite product or service within your company's offerings, encourage them to increase their knowledge of your full line of products and services. Introduce them to new products as they are rolled out. Offer incentives and reward programs.
3.   Veteran salespeople's needs are quite different from the newcomers, and sometimes, as an effective leader, you must provide training that introduces new applications for old products. Broaden the veteran's vision of your company's products and services.
4.   More than ever, your veteran salespeople will need to know their competition as well as they know your company and its products and services.
5.   It's also important to take your veteran salespeople back to the basics

in their training. Give them a time to review the fundamentals. It's a proven fact that exceptional salespeople consistently practice and perform the fundamentals a little bit better than their competitors. That's usually what gives your people the leading edge.

6. Lastly, you'll need to teach your veterans time- and account-management. At this point in their careers, they need to be working every moment to its maximum return and learning to efficiently manage their accounts.

Telemarketers

Your telemarketers may often be the first contact customers have with your company—make that first contact count.

> Train your people well, and your returns will reflect that training.

1. Teach them your product line and/or special services that will differentiate you from your competition.
2. Provide a sales dialogue for your telemarketers that will help them with the prospect's common questions and objections.
3. Most of all, train them to adopt impeccable telephone manners. They will be faced with an incredible amount of negative, and many telemarketers do not have the income potential of your salespeople. If they feel the money doesn't justify their best effort, their poor performance may be a reflection of that attitude. They must be rewarded by being provided all the advantages of excellent training and coaching.

Your marketing support representatives also need to know your product line; they will benefit from training that is specific to their needs.

• Teach them proper verbal demonstration/presentation skills.
• Coach them to be coaches themselves as they educate the customers.
• Train them to apply these selling skills in their specific arena of telemarketing. After all, they are salespeople too, except they are promoting the company, which in turn keeps the company successfully producing for its salespeople.

<u>Managers</u>
Lastly, we have you, the managers—the leaders of your companies. What type of training do you need?
1. First, you'll need basic management skills.
2. Then you'll need to know how to motivate your people.
3. Next, you'll progress to leadership skills.
4. You should be trained on proper reporting techniques.
5. Since most of you came up through the ranks of top producing salespeople, you'll need to have had all that training with an emphasis on advanced product knowledge. After all, it's the manager who is expected to provide the answers to unresolved problems.
6. Effective communications skills are a must.
7. Finally, you'll need to know all the ins and outs of running a branch operation.

Okay, we've covered some of the WHO, now what about the HOW of training. What methods of training are available and when should they be used?

Four Basic Training Models

<u>One-on-One</u>
I once heard someone say that the best classroom was a tree stump in the forest with a wise old man sitting on one end and a student on the other. Barring the comfort aspect, that's probably "one-on-one" at its best. With one-on-one training, the veteran or manager takes the opportunity to personally mentor or supervise the mentoring of the new salesperson. The rookie watches the pro and vice versa. Observation and instruction are the focus of one-on-one training.

<u>Lecturing</u>
Although this method of training is still the most widely used, it has its limitations. It usually follows what the lecturer **wants**—not what the salespeople or support staff **need**. Because of its lack of interaction, the attendees' attention tends to wander during much of the lecture.

<u>Workshops</u>
This type of training is a great way to teach problem-solving principles. It is usually done in groups or teams, which creates a lively, competitive atmosphere.

The interactive learning environment is very conducive to learning and **remembering** new skills.

Combination

Today's companies should be using a combination of all these methods. Depending on the objectives of the training, methods can be varied to accommodate all learning styles and to help teams and individuals accomplish their goals.

No matter what method of training you use, trainers who give assignments and establish regular follow-up programs usually have the most positive results. Today's technology has given us much flexibility in our training. Some follow-up training can be done by satellite, audio/video and through books and company manuals.

What to Look for in a Trainer

Three of the most important aspects of today's trainers are **enthusiasm**, **knowledge** and **hands-on** methods of training.

Those who encourage student involvement and interactive activities are most memorable. I check my programs to make sure that I've included the 3 "R's" (repetition, rehearsal, role-playing). Lastly, your trainer should design within his or her programs a time for you and your people to ask questions. There should be enough flexibility within a model to allow the time necessary to make it company specific by personally addressing the needs of your team.

Once you receive great training, how do you reinforce that training by being a great coach? One of the things you can do is to accompany your salespeople when they call on an account. Tape their presentation and request that your salesperson do a personal evaluation on his or her performance while you do the same. Next, meet with and discuss the salesperson's progress.

It's a good habit to continuously set goals and review them with your salespeople. If their activities do not reflect what's needed to achieve their goals, then adjust their goals or activities to bring them into alignment.

What I did with the people I managed was to set a goal range. We would aim high but set a bottom line goal as well. It would be wonderful to achieve that high goal, but absolutely unthinkable for them to accept anything below their low goal. This was quite helpful when establishing a plan of action. Just a helpful hint—I made it a habit to immediately review goals with my people when they returned from an extended vacation. That is when many salespeople had a difficult time getting back into the groove of successful sales. So, I used it as a time to reinforce proven habits and establish new ones to see them through to their next goal.

How did I reinforce those old habits? It can be as simple as offering praise for a job well done. When was the last time you gave positive stokes to your people? If you expect honesty and integrity to be in your salespeople's program, make them a part of your management style. Treat your salespeople the way you want them to treat your customers. Teach by example.

Develop a strong support system for your people by showing them you care. They'll then do the same in the field with their customers. Respect and expect!

Respect your salespeople and **expect** them to pass that same respect on to their customers. I'm sure you've heard it said before: "Salespeople respect what you inspect."

So, be a trainers' trainer. Inspect their progress and coach them in an effective follow-up program.

Teach yourself to be an outstanding coach by receiving the proper training. Put programs in place that can be continued between workshops and seminars. Keep a learning, working salesperson's library. Ask questions of your own mentors. Study and learn from industry greats. Enthusiastically discuss what you are currently learning as you manage your people, and let them know that you are a believer in lifelong learning.

Seven Winning Character Traits of a Great Manager

1. Reliability

Do what you say you'll do. You'll keep your new recruits and maintain strong, ongoing relationships with your top performers if you deliver what you promise. It's really quite similar to when you were a salesperson making promises to your customers. The difference is that now your customers are your salespeople.

2. <u>Empathy</u>
Be interested in your people's challenges, hopes and aspirations. Notice I said empathy not sympathy. There's a big difference. With empathy you can understand them yet still expect their best performance.

3. <u>Patience</u>
Winning takes time to develop, so be patient. Make your expectations a workable combination between being reasonable and challenging.

4. <u>Honesty</u>
Don't lie to your salespeople or your superiors. This is much easier said than done. When you've had an incredibly bad quarter, it is so tempting to blame others when you know it was your responsibility. And, when you've had an incredibly good quarter, it's so easy to exaggerate the figures and inflate the results because you want to make your people feel good. Give them reality. Be honest with them. It will affect everything they do from here on out, so they need to know the truth of the situation.

5. <u>Industrious</u>
Work as hard as you expect your people to work. Don't ask anything of them that you wouldn't be willing to do.

6. <u>Persistence</u>
This is one of the most valuable traits of all. NEVER GIVE UP! Keep on learning—be on a quest for the best for you and your people.

7. <u>Grace Under Pressure</u>
Maintain your poise. Keep your cool in an emergency. Let your people know you trust them to identify, establish and implement a success plan.

It's no easy job to train and coach your people.

 The more you build strong relationships and partner your efforts with outside trainers, the more effective they can be in helping you to design programs that will meet the specific needs of your people.

Help your people to connect their activities and goals to their dreams—and they'll reward you with great performance.

Working Through the Process--Chapter Eight

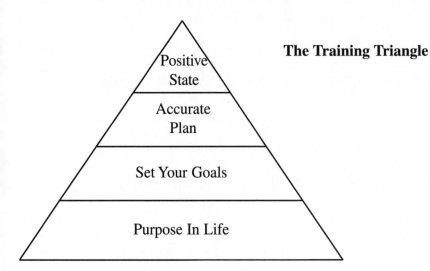

The Training Triangle

1. How do you coach and encourage prospecting?

    _____

    _____

2. How do you teach your people to effectively approach their customers?

    _____

    _____

3. How do you build rapport with your customers to establish long-lasting relationships

    _____

    _____

4. What questioning techniques are most effective during the selling sequence?

5. How do you organize and deliver a powerful presentation/demonstration?

6. How can you handle and overcome even the most challenging objections?

7. What is your plan to implement strong selling skills that get you to the close, and earn the right to ask for the business?

8. When you've done your job well, how do you ask for referrals?

9. How do you sell with integrity and ethics?

10. How do you effectively manage your time and territory?

_____

_____

11. How are you currently facing the challenges of a career in sales?

_____

_____

12. What are you doing to develop telephone strategies with positive results?

_____

_____

❖ What are the benefits of GREAT training?
   1. Greater _____.
   2. Develops _____ work habits by _____ the salesperson's skills.
   3. Raises the salesperson's _____ level.
   4. Raises the salesperson's _____ level.
   5. Creates more _____ customers and long lasting customer _____.
   6. Decreases _____, making the most out of your _____.
   7. It's an excellent _____ tool.

❖ What will you look for in a trainer?

_____

_____

_____

❖ How will you coach new skills?

_____

_____

❖ What will you do to follow-up training?

_____

_____

❖ Seven Point Checklist

   ❏ Have you set up a _____ _____?

   ❏ What will need to be _____? What can you expect in _____?

   ❏ Will this program need to be ____ to your _____? How do you plan to do that?

   ❏ How will this training benefit ___, your _____ and your _____?

   ❏ What is your long-range _____? How will this training help you to turn your _____ into a _____?

   ❏ How will this training address the _____ needs of your team?

   ❏ Does the trainer know your _____?

CHAPTER NINE

Motivation Is Not A Temporary Experience

"The biggest difference between a wisher and a doer is motivation."
Charles "Tremendous" Jones

Chapter Highlights:

▶ Motivating Your Salespeople Out of Mediocrity
▶ Intrinsic vs. Extrinsic Motivation
▶ Helping Your People to Reach Self-Actualization
▶ Behavior of a Great Manager

What do you think of when I say the word "motivation?" Do you think of an athletic coach pumping up his or her team in the locker room before a big game? Or, do you think of a special keynote speaker delivering a rah-rah speech to your salespeople at a beginning-of-the-year conference? Whatever your picture, it usually refers to a short-lived, positive, motivational experience—a temporary high.

Motivation is not a temporary experience. Did you know you are being moved to act or "motivated" every day, and it isn't always in a positive manner? Motivation can be a negative experience as well. Sometimes those negative experiences can be very long-term and leave lots of residual side affects. Because we are so susceptible to other people's influence or the power outside events have on our attitude and behavior, many of us motivate or are motivated without being aware of the experience.

 Whether you motivate or are motivated to act negatively of positively, temporarily or long-term, rah-rah or focused and productive, you experience constant, ongoing motivation.

Think back to a time that you were greatly influenced by an outstanding manager. Perhaps this person was even responsible for encouraging you to enter sales. Are you getting the picture of this person? We all have one in our memory. Did that person seem to have a natural ability to motivate? Sure—and if you can still remember that manager today, I'd say that motivation was fairly long-lasting too. Now, think of a manager or supervisor you had in the past who just rubbed you the wrong way. Perhaps he or she was a poor communicator, never letting you know what was expected of you. Or, maybe the manager you are picturing failed to involve you in any of the decision making and you never had any say in department matters. Was that manager a natural motivator? You don't think of those types of managers as being motivators, but they are.

Motivation is neither positive nor negative. It simply means "The will to act."

Someone or something creates in you a will to act—moves you to create and implement a plan. That someone can even be that little voice in your head. In fact, some of the strongest motivation is that which is within us—both negatively and positively.

You probably never thought of it that way, but YOU listen more to YOUR voice than any other voice in the world. That little voice in your head is talking all the time. You can be sitting in a meeting, looking like you are paying careful attention to what is being discussed, when all the time you are carrying on an inner conversation. You could be discounting everything the presenter is saying. That little voice is saying, "Sure we can make that new quota for the quarter—in a pig's eye, we can! There just aren't enough hours in a day for my salespeople to sleep and work the kind of schedule required to meet that quota."

Or, you might have an executive who is really trying to positively motivate you at a meeting or conference, but just three days ago he or she was calling you on the carpet about your particular method of management. All the rah-rah stuff can't break through the inner voice of resentment.

> This inner conversation is going on in the minds of those you speak to—every day, and it is louder and more powerful than anyone in the room. Multiply that by every person in the meeting, and the noise is deafening—yet not one word is heard—including that of the presenter.

No matter how strong your leadership skills, or how motivating your activities, if you can't break through to that little voice going on in the heads of your people—you don't have a chance to change their behaviors and attitudes. How can you hold yourself totally responsible for motivating your people? It's not just about you; it's about them, too. It's a team effort. I've heard it said before that much of a salesperson's behavior, motivating perceptions and positive beliefs are <u>dependent</u> upon his or her leader's ability to <u>positively</u> and actively motivate them. I say—believe that one and I've got some beachfront property in Nebraska to sell ya!

Oh, it sounds good in theory, but let me explain what I mean. If that were true, then the best managers would always be the most enthusiastically positive or the most negatively controlling, and that just isn't the case. I've been highly motivated by managers that were neither of those. I've watched how some of the managers I've had meant well, but struggled in mediocrity. That's when I made up my mind I would never be that kind of a leader. In fact, I'd say I've been almost just as motivated to accomplish by people who provided examples of poor performance—knowing what they were capable of doing—than I have been inspired by the greats in the industry or devastated by the incredibly poor performers.

There is something within me that just abhors the thought of being "average." Whenever I am exposed to average—average workers, average managers, average relationships, average earnings—whatever—it just gets my hackles up. I guess the reason I dislike average so much is because I'm always thinking: "That person could be so much more. With just a LITTLE more effort or a LITTLE more knowledge and skills, they could be great."

> Most of the time average is only separated from great by a hairline's distance.

If all those average performers only knew how close they were to being great, there isn't a one of them who wouldn't work just a bit harder to achieve greatness.

Within your salespeople and yourself, you have all the motivation you will ever need. It's an untapped treasure buried right in your own backyard. The problem is, you don't know it's there. Or, you don't know how to unlock its riches. And, should you accidentally discover your buried treasure, you fail to recognize its value and leave it out in the backyard for ages. Every time you go by the window you give it a look to make sure it's still there. Sometimes you even go out in the yard and fiddle with the lock to see if for some reason it magically opens. When you get tired of leaving it out in the backyard, you drag your treasure inside and turn it into a nightstand or a TV tray. It becomes just a pretty piece of furniture that you NEVER use to its full potential. After a while, you forget its presence in your life.

I gave you that example because that's how most managers have responded to all the "gems" they've been given by outstanding educators and great motivational leaders. If you're one of those managers, it could be that you've locked up all those productive skills and strategies trainers have taught you throughout the years and buried them in your subconscious. Should someone come along and MOTIVATE you to dig up all those treasures you already have locked away—sure, you would do that. Perhaps you'd take another look at what you've been taught and mess with those little "gems" of information for a short while. Then, when you were unable to successfully unlock all the riches promised by the trainer or educator, you would give up and return to your old style of managing. You might bring little pieces of knowledge into your sales meetings and use it for something other than what it was meant to do, but most of the time all the riches of training have been forgotten by the time you get back to your office.

Make yourself a promise—set a course to use the information you are learning in these pages. Use it immediately. Drag this book into your office and take a reading break while you're having a quick bite at your desk. Take a walk and pop a management session tape into your tape player or portable CD player. Unlock all the treasures offered within these chapters, and internalize as much as you can use to give you a richer, more fulfilling leadership experience. OH, one thing I forgot to mention—the more you take from the treasure, the more your riches multiply. The more you share the wealth of knowledge contained within this book—the richer you and your salespeople become.

Maslow's Hierarchy of Needs

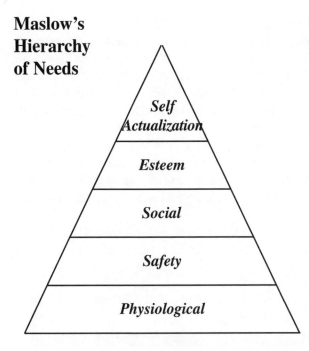

A great model that illustrates motivation is Maslow's Hierarchy of Needs. I'm sure you've all heard of Maslow's pyramid. Let's review it for those of you who may not remember every level. The most basic needs we all have are our <u>physiological needs</u>: warmth, shelter, food—you know, the basics. If you don't have these needs covered, it's very difficult for you to progress to higher levels of achievement. Let me give you an example, have you ever been to a meeting just before lunch and all you can think of is food? That's because you haven't attended to your physiological needs.

Next on Maslow's pyramid is the need for <u>safety</u>, which is really the need for security, or the absence of fear. I can almost guarantee you that you could be in the middle of one of the most interesting seminars ever, and one little mouse scurrying around on the floor could change the entire learning environment. Many people have a great fear of mice and would have an immediate shift in needs.

The third level on Maslow's pyramid is our <u>social needs</u>. I don't care how much of a loner you are, there is a innate need within you to have friends, to experience a sense of belonging. This is a very powerful need for many salespeople. Sometimes this need is so over-powering that they will fail to close the sale because they fear ruining the relationship they've built with the prospect. Or, often times members of your sales team will have such a strong need to feel a part of the group that they will choose lunch with the group rather than the isolation of prospecting. While that is okay some of the time, if this becomes their routine, you can be sure they are stuck at the social level. Sadly, some never get any further up Maslow's pyramid.

The next level is <u>esteem needs</u>. This is when you have a great desire or need to be well regarded by others—a need to be appreciated. That is another stumbling block for many in sales. Even many managers have stopped at this level because it's more important for you to be held in high regard than to develop your people. You become the best buddy of some of your salespeople, instead of maintaining the professional distance you need to be an effective leader. Because you want to be held in high regard by your salespeople, you are unwilling to hold potential top performers accountable when they aren't doing the basics—aren't performing at a level you know them capable of achieving. Believe me, they will appreciate you all the more when you do whatever it takes to get them back on track.

Lastly, we have the need for <u>self-actualization</u>. If you are satisfied with being average, you will never have to worry about this level. Average managers never make it to this level. They never realize their potential, and neither do many of their people. They never achieve all they are capable of achieving because they are distracted by all those other needs.

Let me warn you, once you fulfill your need for self-actualization, there's no turning back. Why? Because there is no better feeling, no greater need than to become your best, and help every member on your sales team to do the same.

Talk about motivating—SUCCESS IS THE GREATEST MOTIVATOR IN THE WORLD!

Intrinsic Motivation

All that I have talked about so far is what is known as intrinsic, or inner, motivation. This is the motivation that is within each of us—the ability we have to talk ourselves into getting out of bed in the morning and exercising, when we'd really like to roll over and sleep an extra hour. This is the inner motivation that encourages your salespeople to keep selling, even when they've met their sales goals or quotas and are only one month into the quarter. It's intrinsic motivation, that little voice within, that takes all the information we feed it, interprets it—whether correctly or not, and speaks to us constantly about how we "should" behave and believe.

The key phrase to that last sentence is "whether correctly or not." Sometimes, in fact, I'd say most of the time, our inner voice is sadly mistaken. If it's telling you that you "CAN'T" accomplish and you choose to listen, then guess what? Chances are you are not going to accomplish. On the other hand, even if it's regarding a goal that everybody thinks you'll never achieve, like mine of becoming a millionaire by the time I was 31, if that voice within keeps giving you positive feedback, there's a much better chance you will accomplish your goal.

Extrinsic Motivation

Now that we understand a little more about inner motivation, let's take a look at extrinsic, or outside motivation. That's where you can have great influence in the lives of all those around you. There are really two types of extrinsic motivation: general and focused. Here are the differences:

General Motivation

These types of outside motivators are more visible and obvious than others, and they usually require more conformity. For your salespeople, general motivation is based on perceptions of you and the company. It's influenced further by the salesperson's own inner beliefs and how those beliefs are challenged or affirmed by you and your company's philosophy and culture. This type of motivation is an overall morale builder within your company, your style and method of management, and by the dynamics of your sales team.

Focused Motivation

Focused motivation is individual or team specific. It is the ability to move your people based on the degree to which you can satisfy their identified needs, wants and issues. Focused motivation is a bit more privately communicated. You move your people by being flexible to each one's personality style, instead of expecting them to adapt to yours. You listen more than you tell. You respond rather than react. You discover rather than dictate! That's how you achieve focused motivation with your sales team.

This type of motivation requires that most managers motivate themselves first. It's an ongoing learning process. Think of general motivation as the bigger picture of your entire team, and focused motivation as a one-on-one examination and evaluation of how to motivate each individual member on that team.

Based on more specifically identified needs, wants and issues determined by an observant, aware, proactive leader like yourself, this type of motivation can be as different as the many styles of management or leadership. When you become a focused motivator, it's a two-way street. Once positively motivated, your team will turn around and move you to reach greater accomplishments as well. Speaking of two-way streets—I picture motivation as an intersection in that two-way street. Let me give you an illustration of who is responsible for motivating your sales team.

Everybody plays a part in motivating the team. Let's picture that motivational intersection.

Motivational Intersection

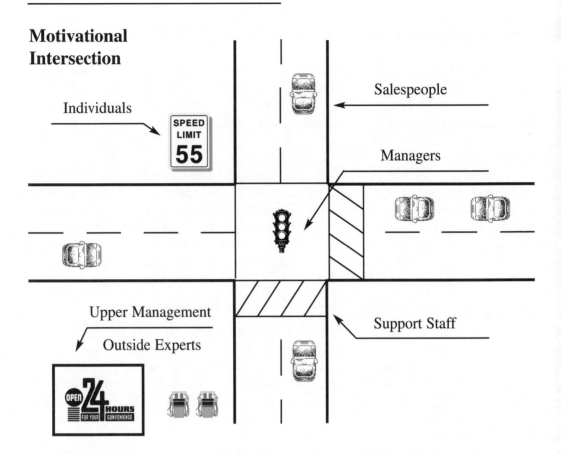

Individuals

Salespeople

Managers

Upper Management

Outside Experts

Support Staff

Managers

Managers are your traffic lights. It's their leadership that signals the success or setbacks of their sales force. They are key to determining the efficient movement of project traffic.

Salespeople

Salespeople are the vehicles. They carry the projects to completion. It's the salespeople who make the numbers happen.

Upper Management/Outside Experts

These people are your corner stations and convenience stores. They offer the necessary fuel and quick energy to your salespeople.

Support Staff
Support Staff are your crosswalks, turn lanes and painted lines. They organize your department and make sure everything runs smoothly. It's your support staff who handle the flow of communications, tasks and projects.

The Individual
The individual represents YOU. You know what is expected of you. You are responsible to hold yourself personally accountable for your own actions and beliefs.

There you have the motivational intersection! Now that I've shown you how the motivational chain works, ask yourself what kind of manager or leader you are.

Are You a Manager Who Controls or a Leader Who Encourages Self-Actualization?

- Do you feel like you have to constantly drive your salespeople to achieve your benchmarks? Or, do you offer help to those struggling to achieve their individual goals and reinforce their importance to the team?

- Do you play the heavy and even go so far as to fire salespeople in order to put fear into the others and get the job done? Or, do you identify areas of improvement in your team and provide additional training, coaching and mentoring?

- Do you consider yourself the decision-maker? Or, do you see yourself as a facilitator, asking for suggestions and ideas and ways to implement them from your salespeople?

- Do you hold yourself responsible for your salespeople's morale? Or, do you expect and encourage your people to evaluate themselves and discover their own solutions?

- Finally, do you feel like you should hold yourself apart from your salespeople, refusing to make yourself available to them, in order to maintain a chain of command? Or, do you prefer open and involved, hands-on leadership?

If most of you believe the second options fit your style of management better, you're well on your way to establishing an efficient, productive, no-blame work environment. An environment designed to create peak performers out of the majority of your people. I say majority because there are some who could care less whether they produce or not, and they will eventually leave your organization.

I once knew a woman who was given an opportunity to manage a regional team of salespeople. This was at a time when it was rare for women to hold a manager's position, and she was eager to do well and a little anxious to begin her career in management. Although she came up through the ranks of salespeople and understood the challenges they faced, she had been a part of an incredibly motivated team—a team that focused on encouraging one another, working hard and taking advantage of ongoing educational opportunities. She bloomed under the management style of a leader who believed in positive feedback, trusting his salespeople to participate in the decision-making process, and coaching them to become their best. From there she went on to become a strong leader herself, and was well on her way to a wonderful career in upper management.

When the company transferred her to another part of the country and offered her the position of regional sales manager, she was ready to pass on all she had learned to her team. What a shock she had when she moved, to find that the only thing she couldn't "move" was the team of salespeople in her new region. Eighty salespeople—and none willing to do what it took to create their own success.

She had a tough decision to face. She could spend months trying to motivate them, but the region was falling so far behind; she feared there was no time to lose. So, she made a gutsy move. With their next check she included a pink slip—all eighty were fired that Friday. She included a letter in the checks stating that resumes were being accepted Monday for any that cared to apply. However, the fired employees were not the only ones sweating it out that weekend. On Monday, fifty-seven workers came back and achieved a 17 percent increase that year. Sometimes it takes that kind of courage and belief in yourself to turn a team around, to be the leader they need to enable your team to become their best. What about you? What are your goals for you and your team? What are you willing to do to achieve those goals?

Create the Cooperation of a Winning Sales Team

- Expect to give cooperation first and your salespeople will be more willing to return it.

- Be genuinely cheerful and accepting of the mistakes your salespeople may make while learning new skills and strategies.
- Provide incentives, rewards and praise for work well done.
- Develop a progressive plan—share your ideas at morale-boosting meetings.
- Publicly recognize your people through bulletin boards, or perhaps through broadcast e-mails and faxes.
- Ask for suggestions. Many managers have a suggestions box outside their office that welcomes the concerns of their salespeople to be given and discussed at the next sales meeting.
- Set high targets for challenging tasks. This keeps peak performers interested while it builds and stretches the up and coming salespeople.
- Appreciate the differences of each member of your team. Communicate your beliefs about the importance of each one's contribution.

Great Managers Do a Lot More Looking than Talking

Take a look at where you team is now and then determine where you would like to lead them. What is the overall attitude of your people? Are they cheerful and efficient, or do they seem more stressed and disorganized? If so, then you should be asking yourself what you can do as a manager to help motivate them to change their behaviors and attitudes.

> Great managers do a lot more looking than talking.

They observe their salespeople's facial expressions and body language to see if it is in harmony with their words. For example, if the salesperson responds to the question of "How are you doing?" with your typical "Oh, fine. I'm doing fine," the savvy manager observes that salesperson's expression as he or she talks on the phone, and the body language as that salesperson sit in a sales meeting. If the nonverbal communication is sending a different signal than his or her verbal responses, the manager knows THERE IS WORK TO BE DONE.

The effective manager and leader listens to the responses of their salespeople.

What do their salespeople's voices sound like? Are they enthusiastic and excited about what they are doing? If not, that manager knows there are some needs there that aren't being met—THEY'VE GOT WORK TO DO.

Observant managers know whether or not their people have the hearts for selling.

Do they have that certain spark that lets the customers know they love what they do? Do they energize the selling atmosphere? If not—the manager knows—THERE IS WORK TO BE DONE.

What about your sales teams? Do you need to speak privately with some of your salespeople? Do you need to get out of your office and go out in the field or on the floor with your salespeople and experience first-hand what they do every day? Do you need to discover if they have some personal problems that are inhibiting their ability to close the sale? If so—THERE IS WORK TO BE DONE.

REMEMBER, THERE IS NOTHING LIKE SUCCESS TO MOTIVATE YOUR SALES TEAM.

Working Through the Process--Chapter Nine

❖ Characteristics of the two types of motivation: general and focused motivation

General Motivation:

1. _____ morale building within your company and sales team.

2. Based on your salespeople's _____ of company _____ and
   _____.

3. Non-specific motivation--but more _____, more _____, more
   _____.

Focused Motivation:

1. _____ or ____ specific--people are moved based on your ability
   to _____ their _____ needs, wants and issues.

2. This type of motivation is usually _____ communicated.

3. It is dependent upon your ability to be _____ to your people's
   _____ _____ instead of expecting them to adapt to yours.

4. Requires that most managers _____ themselves first--following
   ongoing _____ programs to become better leaders.

❖ When you hear the word "motivation," what is your picture?

_____

_____

❖ Who does the motivating on your team?

_____

❖ What types of motivation work best for your salespeople?

_____

_____

❖ How do you motivate your team? Its individuals?
Team:

_____

_____

Individuals:

_____

_____

❖ What kind of manager or leader are you?
  1. Do you feel as though you have to _____ your salespeople constantly in order to _____ your _____?
  2. Do you play the _____ and even go so far as to ____ in order to get the job done?
  3. Do you consider yourself _____ to be the _____-_____?
  4. Do you hold yourself totally responsible for the _____ of your salespeople?
  5. Do you feel you should _____ yourself from your salespeople in order to maintain an effective _____ of _____?

  NOTE: If you answered YES to the above questions, you are following _____ form of management, and you're in danger of _____ your top people to more _____ leaders in your industry!

❖ Looking back on the methods you've used to motivate yourself and others, would you say you used more negative or positive forms of motivation? Explain.

Negative:

_____

_____

Positive:

_____

_____

❖ Three NEVERS managers ALWAYS want to remember.
1. NEVER make _____ you don't intend to keep. It will ALWAYS _____ your people.
2. NEVER ___ _____ to do what you wouldn't do. It will ALWAYS cause _____ in your people.
3. NEVER ___ with _____ to one sharing innovative ideas. It will ALWAYS _____ future _____ of other team members.

❖ Where is your team now? Where would you like them to be? What is your motivational plan?

Current status:

_____

_____

Future status:

_____

_____

Motivational Plan:

_____

_____

CHAPTER TEN

Salesperson's Dream or Manager's Disaster?

"If you're sitting on the bleachers of management rather than leading your team to victory, you're probably on the butt-end of this season's success."
Omar Periu

Chapter Highlights:

▶ Identifying, Developing, Measuring and Rewarding Outstanding Behavior
▶ Evaluation Commitment Form
▶ Establishing Effective Incentives and Rewards
▶ NAACP Involvement
▶ Making it Fun

Whenever you consider motivation, especially extrinsic (outside) influences, you cannot avoid covering rewards, incentives and contests. Rewards, incentives and contests can be a salesperson's dream and a manager's disaster. As critical as these things can be to a salesperson's performance, if inappropriate, they can backfire and cause long-lasting, unexpected, negative results. Since nobody likes ugly surprises, here is some helpful information about contests, incentives and rewards.

Before you can offer any of them, you've got to know what behaviors and performance you want to measure, how you're going to measure it, and then you can sit back and worry about the results these incentives and rewards will bring.

It's a known fact that what you IDENTIFY, DEVELOP, MEASURE and REWARD is what will be reinforced in your sales force.

Unfortunately, it works with both the negative and positive behaviors.

Let me explain a little further what is meant by IDENTIFY, DEVELOP, MEASURE and REWARD.

Identify

As a manager, it's up to you to identify your salespeople's strengths and areas of improvement. There are three phases to this identifying process.

Phase One: Know the strengths and weaknesses of your individual salespeople.

Phase Two: Discover how those strengths and weaknesses will affect the performance of the team.

Phase Three: Take a look at the strengths and weaknesses of your entire team, not just the extremes—the most and least productive. In doing so, you should get a clear picture of the working dynamics of your people as a whole.

Once you have identified these three phases, you will be ready to move into DEVELOPMENT.

Develop

Focus on developing a great working environment and strong relationships between you and your salespeople.

Salespeople are a manager's customers, so learning to provide quality customer service should be number one on a manager's list of priorities.

One of the best ways to develop a strong team is to encourage your people to make a commitment to a common goal or objective and then work hard to achieve that goal. There's nothing more motivating than planned achievement where each team member actually contributes to the success of the whole.

It's a good idea to have each salesperson authorize a commitment form that will hold them accountable to do what it takes to be successful. At the same time, you make a commitment ON PAPER to invest your time and money to develop your people. Why make a commitment in writing? Well, what you agree to and authorize in writing seems to give you more determination to achieve, and you have your commitments on paper to remind you of your original promises when times get tough and enthusiasm runs low. It's also much easier to measure exactly what you will reward when you have your planned achievement written down. Below is an Evaluation Commitment form you may want to use with your people:

EVALUATION COMMITMENT FORM

This agreement to commit is effective through this _____ day of _____ (WRITE DOWN THE DATE OF YOUR NEXT EVALUATION). Upon discussion with and evaluation of the below authorized witness, mentor and/or manager, I promise to continue my efforts and establish myself as a believer in (INSERT COMPANY NAME) philosophies and objectives in order to create an unbeatable team!

Based on my performance discussed in this evaluation dated _____, I plan to work hard to improve these three things. (CHOOSE THREE ITEMS YOU AND YOUR SALESPERSON DISCUSSED THAT NEEDED IMPROVEMENT.)

1. _____
2. _____
3. _____

I, (INSERT MANAGER'S NAME), commit to doing whatever it takes to help (INSERT NAME OF SALESPERSON) achieve improvement in the above areas. As discussed in the evaluation process, I commit to doing the following three things to help (INSERT NAME OF SALESPERSON) reach success:

1. _____
2. _____
3. _____

Together, we plan to measure the success of our commitments through the following method:

_____

_____

_____

_____

Together we promise IN WRITING to positively encourage and support each other's efforts and performance as attested by the following dated signatures.

_____   _____
            Salesperson   Date

_____   _____
             Manager   Date

Measure

This is the area of accountability. As a manager, you are ultimately responsible for the performance of your team. However, if everybody doesn't buy into your program, philosophy, goals and objectives, none of you are going very far. Exceptional leaders know to hold themselves accountable, as well as their salespeople and the entire sales team—for both the setbacks and successes.

If you're going to hold everybody accountable, communication is the key. For example, how will you be able to hold your salespeople accountable for behaviors and activities that you never clearly communicated to them ? It could have been that you told them what you expected but forgot to educate them on what would be considered average versus outstanding performance.

One of the best ways to encourage salespeople to work at their peak is for managers to reinforce the behaviors and actions they want to see continued. That's where contests, incentives and rewards are important. The challenge for managers is to make sure the behaviors and actions you are reinforcing are the RIGHT ones. Many times, what happens is that we unintentionally reward the wrong behavior.

The difference is so slight that it goes unnoticed for a while. The next thing you know, you lose a top producer because you set up an unhealthy competition between your top producers and their peers.
Here are a few things to keep in mind when measuring your success.
1. Make sure that every salesperson believes he or she has an equal chance to achieve what is being measured.
2. Plan carefully what is being measured and how that measurement will be judged for success. When you practice careful planning, you will be less likely to create a negative work environment or unhealthy competition between your salespeople.
3. Communicate what will be measured and when that measurement will occur. The "when" is an important ingredient in the measurement formula. If salespeople know what is being measured but fail to understand the time frame, they may miss the mark because of a miscommunication.
4. One of the best standards of measurement is a salesperson's own best production. When the competition is against your own best self, it rarely acts as a demotivator to others—everybody wins.

While being attentive to the needs of your team, managers cannot ignore the wants of the individual. Often times a manager waits until his or her salespeople resort to greatly reduced sales figures or poor performance before reaching out to the individual and together discovering ways to work through his or her personal challenges. Another popular thing for managers to do is to create incentives, contests and/or rewards when performance slumps, which in turn can send a message to their sales team that poor performance generates rewards in the form of additional bonuses and the celebration of mediocrity. Let's talk about rewards and their results.

Rewards

Rewards show your appreciation of a job well done—either monetarily or through some other form, like public recognition, special gifts, a day off with pay, a weekend away on the company, etc…

 Whatever you decide to use as rewards and incentives, make sure they are reinforcing the behaviors you want to see continued. Easier said than done!

What kinds of contests, incentives and rewards will best motivate your salespeople? It's about as varied as any individual on your sales team is different from any other. But, I'll give you some suggestions just to get your creativity going. What you really want to do is know your salespeople well enough to know what personally motivates them, then tailor your incentives and rewards to the individual.

Suggested Incentives and Rewards

What you can offer is a variety of things and allow your salespeople to choose. Perhaps it's a day of pampering at the local spa, complete with massage and time in the tanning booth. Or, maybe it's a pair of movie or sporting event passes with a personalized letter stating how much you appreciate their extra effort to achieve your team's goal.

- When bonus money or raises are not available, you can still provide incentives and rewards through praise and appreciation. Stop by a person's office when you know they'll have a meeting with their co-workers and tell them you just wanted to extend a special thanks. Recognize them in front of their peers at the next sales meeting. Remember, rewards and incentives don't always have to be about money.
- Consider training as an incentive for your people. It's one of the only incentives or rewards that offer incredible returns on your investment. Make it a privilege to receive a paid experience attending a special workshop or seminar. Or, the next time you are at a great seminar, decide to own some of their products. Take a few extras to reward the exceptional behavior of members of your team.

Let me share with you a story about a contest set up by a manager who ended up creating such a negative situation that he lost two of his top producers. He organized a contest that he thought would offer everybody an equal chance to achieve success. It was based on each member increasing their annual productivity by 10 percent. To this manager, looking at most everybody on his team, a 10 percent increase sounded quite attainable. What he failed to consider was his two top producers who were working at their maximum—and then some. Ten percent for them was next to impossible to achieve. He failed to consider that 10 percent of millions was much more difficult to achieve than a 10 percent increase at the bottom realm. Because his two top producers were over-achievers, they sacrificed family, personal goals and even their health to achieve success. What happened was major burnout. One of his top producers decided to retire that year, and the other moved over to the competition where she felt she'd be more appreciated.

Here are some tips on how to establish appropriate and effective incentives and rewards.

Tip #1

Make your rewards and incentives specific to the individual and then align them with the team's goals and objectives.

Tip #2

Make your rewards and incentives directly proportionate to the individual effort of the recipient. If several people were involved and you would like all to be rewarded for their efforts, realize that the rewards and incentives don't necessarily have to be equally distributed. I call these my NAACP exceptions because it's a time when it's okay to be UNEQUAL, to reward UNEQUAL efforts. Okay, some of you may recognize those initials to stand for another organization, but this is how I see it regarding the reinforcement of the behaviors I want to see continued.

Get the NAACP Involved

N = NEW. New ideas and innovative suggestions were very valuable to my team when I was managing, so the "N" stood for NEW!

A = ACTION. I have always been a believer in the development of an effective plan of ACTION. And, I rewarded that behavior.

A = ANCHOR. Sometimes you have to take that creativity and innovative nature and ANCHOR it to a more traditional school of thought. So, when the more traditional thinkers would offer ways to do that, they were rewarded as well.

C = COURAGE and CONFIDENCE. Changing behaviors that are comfortable often requires a lot of COURAGE and CONFIDENCE. Because many team efforts are based on change, it's good to get your people thinking positively about change—with COURAGE and CONFIDENCE.

P = PREPARATION. It isn't enough to know, or to apply what you know to what you do, but, rather, you have to prepare yourself to handle the changes. When I witnessed a salesperson preparing him/herself for success, I really wanted to reward that behavior. Remember, as a manager, if you are stingy with your incentives and rewards, your people will be stingy with their performance and achievements. In the meantime, as you are deciding on what incentives and rewards to use, keep an eye out for the competition. Not competition outside your organization, but the competition you might arbitrarily set up between the members on your own team through mistaken incentives, ineffective rewards, or overly competitive contests.

 Find ways for everybody to win—not just your top or bottom-level producers.

Polarized rewards can create polarized teams. You may want to have salespeople who are especially great at customer service share with the team an effective tool they use that is highly successful. Or, have another salesperson share what they learned through studying one of the experts whose works you have in your department sales library.

This was a clever idea. I heard of one manager who held an incentive lottery. When his entire team's performance and efforts jumped up 5 percent, he would have a random drawing and give a prize to one of the participating salespeople.

Make it FUN!

Whatever your contest, incentive or reward—MAKE IT FUN.

Make your salespeople eager to participate and they'll do whatever it takes to successfully achieve your team's objectives and goals. Have a good time, and nobody will want to miss out on all the fun.

There are many types of incentives and rewards. Discover what works for individual salespeople and for the entire team as well. Here are some of the categories of rewards and incentives to consider:

- Recognition
- Money
- Health and Family Benefits
- Group Insurance with the Company
- Travel or Training
- Feedback
- Personal Appreciation through a Private Meeting, Lunch or a Letter or Personalized Note

About those cash rewards! Non-financial rewards can be as varied as your imaginations will allow, but what about cash rewards? The following are a few ways to create monetary rewards in the form of special gifts.

- <u>Salary increases that are reflected in base pay</u>. Like a merit pay—this monetary reward is long lasting and very memorable. It just keeps on saying "Thanks."

> A warning when you give salary increases based on merit—your salespeople may disagree with the amount your company is willing to pay for their efforts, and the reward or pay increase incentive can come back to haunt you.

Some people are definitely not motivated strictly by money. Money can't give them   a dream picture to work toward like that exotic vacation or fancy little sports car. To some, making more money just means that more goes out in bills. While that's good, it isn't very inspiring.

If you give salary or monetary rewards and incentives, make sure you reinforce their dreams in the process. For example, if you know that your salesperson would love to own a new ski boat, link that dream to the monetary rewards you offer. Include two passes to the boat show with their first pay increase. Make sure you include a personalized note that says something about the fact that you are counting on this to help them fund their dream of owning a ski boat. That lets them know you are listening to their dreams, and that their dreams are important to you.

It's personal—more caring, and it gets them focused on their dreams and what they need to do to achieve those dreams. If not, all you may have achieved is a salesperson focused on money received that must be taken home to pay down on a credit card. For most people this is NOT what dreams are made of.

- <u>Commissions and Bonuses</u>: These are one-time payments that reflect successful achievement of goals. Be careful with these though. It's a good idea to start out small with these types of rewards and give yourself room to increase the reward. Also, don't just depend on holiday bonuses or your salespeople will learn to do the same. Make it a practice to offer bonuses only when the performance was really special.

> Avoid rewarding with bonuses regularly at the holiday times; salespeople begin to associate the bonus with the season instead of the effort.

Lastly, it may be a mistake to offer equal bonuses to all salespeople at the same time of year. Instead of an incentive for the salespeople, it could become a burden for the company.

Let me explain—not every salesperson is working at the same pace, level of expertise or rate of success. Your umbrella bonus may actually come at a time when that particular salesperson has exhibited no behavior or extraordinary performance that merits a bonus. So, what message are you sending with your general bonus. First of all, the untimely bonus may say that you are not aware of their individual efforts, or that you don't see them as individuals. And, because you don't, when their performance and behavior DOES merit a special bonus, you're not going to be aware of those times either. Although bonuses should be for everybody, because that is what separates them from performance-related pay, they can be given to all salespeople at the same time, but vary in the amounts.

- <u>Performance-related pay</u>: This is a raise based on outstanding performance. Again, this is ongoing and continuous. In most cases, managers offer performance-related pay at the time they review the salesperson. Much of the time, it's too little, too late.

> Try awarding performance-related pay at the time you first become aware of the desired performance.

Give the behavior a little time to season and form a positive habit, then offer part of the merit pay right on the spot. It doesn't hurt to let them know that the rest of performance pay will come when the task is completed.

One last word to say about rewards, incentives and contests—it takes a lot of visionary planning to achieve the desired results.

> Involve your team in the planning stages of your rewards, incentives and contests; it will give them ownership and stronger commitment to their achievement.

Don't expect positive rewards, incentives and contests to be easy to plan or carry out. You may have to organize a planning and/or design task team and let your people actively participate. It will make your job much easier and more effective when offering rewards and incentives. I'll leave you with this—the MOST important thing to remember is to make your people feel valued and appreciated.

Working Through the Process--Chapter Ten

❖ What rewards and incentives, both individually and with your entire team, have you established in the past 12 months?

Rewards:

_____

_____

Incentives:

_____

_____

❖ Did these rewards and incentives increase or inhibit productivity? Explain!

_____

_____

_____

❖ What type of incentives and rewards during the last 12 months offered the most effective results? Why?

_____

_____

_____

❖ What **non-monetary** rewards and incentives do you plan on using in the next 12 months? What **monetary** rewards and incentives will you use during the next 12 months?

Non-monetary rewards and incentives:

_____

_____

Monetary rewards and incentives:

_____

_____

❖ How will you celebrate you and your team's successes?

_____

_____

_____

CHAPTER ELEVEN

Do It or Delegate It?

"To every person there comes that special moment when he is tapped on the shoulder to do a very special thing unique to him. What a tragedy if that moment finds him unprepared for the work that would be his finest hour."

Winston Churchill

Chapter Highlights:

▶ Why Delegate?

▶ When to Delegate?

▶ The Steps to Delegating

▶ The Costs of Avoiding Delegation

▶ Delegation Form

Although we have heard the word "delegation" since the beginning of our management careers, many do not consistently practice effective delegation. Before we get any further into this chapter, I'd like to first define delegation. Delegation is simply entrusting another person with a task for which the delegator remains ultimately responsible. The end part of that last sentence "for which the delegator remains ultimately responsible" is what holds many managers back from practicing effective delegation. I'll discuss in greater detail later in the chapter some of the barriers to being an effective delegator, and there are plenty. However, those barriers don't have to be prohibitive to effective delegating.

One of the things managers develop who successfully delegate are mechanisms and organized systems for reporting and control. Let's face it, if you are the one to be ultimately responsible, you'll be the one to make sure the project or task delegated is being completed as scheduled. It's your duty to establish standards of quality control, and to make sure that the challenges are not being ignored or that corners are not being cut in order to meet the deadline. After all, managers are responsible for the work of their people; if the work is inferior, your careers are on the line as well as those of your salespeople.

When I was in management, I always thought as if I had to put my stamp of approval, or signature, on everything that came through my office. Wouldn't that be a great thing to instill in your people? How much differently would their performances be if their signatures had to go on all of their work? What if every package delivered right on time to a customer had the name of the delivery person who went the extra mile to meet company standards and do everything possible to deliver that package on time? Right beside their name would be a number of all the times they succeeded in delivering on time. Wow! Would that be a boost, or what?

What if salespeople had to print on their business cards how many times they promised things and successfully delivered what they promised? What if, right there on their agreements was a number indicating to the customer how many times they successfully served their customers? Pretty powerful stuff, wouldn't you say? We all ought to think of it that way—that everything that moves through our office would be broadcast over CNN that evening. It would certainly make you think about how you are treating your people or doing your job as manager, wouldn't it?

No matter how small the task or major the project, much of your work needs to be delegated so that you can focus on developing your team into a MASSIVE ACTION machine. If you have never considered yourself a good delegator, you may want to begin with the smaller tasks that are easier for you to let go of. If it is difficult for you to trust others to do the work, then begin with the little things and build up to the bigger projects. Once you see a line of success with your delegation, you'll be more and more encouraged to continue the process.

Why Delegate Anyway?

First of all, proper delegation increases your time to focus on developing your people. If you've recruited and developed a team of professionals, let them do their job. If you can give a long-term project to a team of experts who will complete the work more efficiently and effectively, why not delegate?

> Delegating also boosts staff morale, builds confidence and reduces stress. There is almost nothing more that a manager can do to show faith in his or her salespeople than to entrust them with an important project.

When they know you believe them capable of doing a great job on the project, your team will rise to the occasion. That's the rewarding thing about delegating—if you expect great successes, you will most often get what you expect.

Harry De Leyer provides us with a perfect example of the truth of that statement. He was the owner and trainer of the legendary "Snow Man," a great standing gray-white horse that Harry bought at the auction when he recognized its ability to become a winner. Together Snow Man and Harry shared a wonderful expectation, one that they knew would some day be just as obvious to others. You see, when Harry first saw Snow Man, he saw beyond the bony legs, matted main and scarred hide. He recognized the championship attitude and fiery passion of the horse. Snow Man recognized in Harry the ability the man had to bring out the best in him, and Snow Man would follow no other. Sure enough, their expectations bore the fruit of their joint efforts when Snow Man was awarded "Horse of the Year" in the Nationals at Madison Square Garden two years in a row. What a shame it would have been if the only other bidder at the auction had won, for his plan was to make glue of the outstanding champion horse. He just didn't have the same expectation from Snow Man. In either case, the horse would have lived or died by its owner's expectations.

Proper delegation is also a stress reducer; it works both for the managers and their teams. Let me explain. If you are stressed to the max because you are overworked, how do you think your salespeople are going to feel? All the stress just spills over to your salespeople. If they need to come to you with a major problem, they are less likely to do so because your time is stretched to the limits and most of the time you are growling like a bear with a sore paw. As a result, their performance may drop off and the stress just keeps on coming. Because the salesperson's performance is dropping, so is his or her income. Before long the situation creates even greater stress for the salesperson and his or her manager.

When a salesperson's performance level falls into a slump, it takes a hit on his or her confidence. What do you think happens to their closing ratios? A customer can smell a desperate salesperson a mile off. If the sale is closed, it's usually done so at a discounted rate with promises that will be difficult if not impossible to keep. All because the salesperson didn't have the confidence to rely on his or her selling skills to close the sale. But it really goes back farther than that—all because you were too busy or stressed by refusing to delegate, and, consequently, didn't take the time to be a supportive coach.

Are You a DOING Manager or a MANAGER'S Manager?

A DOING manager is a manager who has to have his or her hands on everything, sometimes including cleaning retail or visual aids for the field salespeople—they stay just too involved. Research shows these people experience heavy burnout! The MANAGER'S manager is someone who focuses on recruiting, training and retaining top salespeople. They are the ones who move up in the company because they are focusing on what will help their people be better people and thereby become better employees. That's what they are hired to do.

I'm sure all of you have felt the stress of being expected to perform 15 million things at one time, and none of them include what you really need to do to become a proactive manager: strategic, visionary planning and training your people. If you fail to delegate, you'll spend most of your days putting out fires instead of developing an "on fire" sales team.

When to Delegate

If you're convinced you need to be a better delegator, you may be asking yourself "When do I delegate?" Let me give you some clues. The following questions will direct you as to WHEN is the best time to delegate:

1. How much of your time is spent on things that should be delegated? If highly successful leaders spend 90 percent of their days in visionary planning, and you are only able to spend 20 percent, it's time to delegate.
2. Do you have your paperwork under control? Much of a manager's paperwork can be delegated and done more accurately and completely by those more able and talented than the manager. Your delegates will appreciate being trusted with the additional responsibility if they are valued and properly rewarded.
3. How much spare work is there in your department? There is more to sales than making the sale. There is paperwork, meetings, inventory, distribution, customer service, etc. . . Who has more time and could even be more qualified to do that work than you?

Take a close look at your desk; is it piled with stacks of paperwork that are beginning to take root because you've been too busy to give them the attention they need? If so, you've waited too long to delegate. Don't wait until your desk overflows with tasks, and you're still under the gun, still feeling the stress because you are waiting until you have to pass on a project that is already impossible to do on time.

When you wait that long, it forces you to give it to the delegate with unrealistic expectations. Demand that it be accomplished within a time frame that is next to impossible to achieve, and your people won't feel challenged—they'll feel burdened and stressed. Instead of delegating a challenging project, all you've done is delegate the stress. Bad practice!

Speaking of challenging your people, this is a great time to delegate— when your people need to experience a challenge, conquer a new frontier. Delegate a project or task in which your salespeople will feel rewarded when they accomplish—both monetarily and emotionally.

> Delegate tasks that push your salespeople to the limits of what they previously believed themselves capable of doing. Once they have experienced success in just one of those projects, they will be ready to accept the next challenge.

Another time to delegate is when you are unable to prioritize important projects because you have allowed the routine tasks to get in the way of your bigger accomplishments. Delegate what you consider routine tasks to those you know will appreciate your trust and bloom under your mentoring. You never know, what is routine for you may challenge another. What is humdrum for you might give someone with a different personality type a thrill to achieve.

For example, I once knew a manager who never planned team social events because he didn't have the time to make all the arrangements and he didn't want to push that responsibility off on one of his salespeople. Finally, a gentleman on the team put together a holiday party. Everybody had a great time, including the salesperson who did the planning. As soon as the manager realized that fact, he delegated to that salesperson the following:

- Social gatherings for the team
- Awards banquets
- Sales meeting agendas that required the input of all the sales team
- Keeping a calendar of special events that needed planning, including the birthdays of his people

Not only did his team members feel recognized at times when their performance was outstanding, and on special occasions like their birthdays, but they grew much closer as a team. Just being able to delegate those responsibilities to the salesperson who enjoyed the planning of the events took a great load off the mind of the manager. What the manager considered routine was actually exciting to the salesperson to whom he delegated. The salesperson also received the reward of appreciation and recognition from his team as well as his manager.

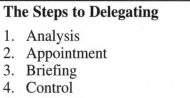

The Steps to Delegating
1. Analysis
2. Appointment
3. Briefing
4. Control
5. Appraisal

Now let me break them down for you one step at a time.

Step #1:   Analysis
During this phase of delegation, a manager sorts through the tasks to be delegated. The following are some of the questions they must ask in order to analyze the tasks:
1. What takes first priority?
2. What are some of the longer projects that will need to be accomplished by a team of salespeople?
3. What tasks require the manager's attention first to gather information that can be passed on to another for more effective delegation?
4. What things cannot be delegated?
   This first step requires each manager to make an action plan.

Step #2:   Appointment
Okay, you've decided what you need to delegate, now is the time to decide who to entrust with the tasks. This is why it is so important to know your team. You'll need to know . . .
- Individual strengths and weaknesses
- Who works well together
- Different personality types and how those will influence task completion

You may be thinking, "Omar, isn't that going a bit too far—personality types?" Absolutely not! How much do you think an entire team of SOCIAL personality types are going to get done with no DRIVER personality types demanding efficient and effective decisions to be made and no ANALYTICAL personality types to point out the facts? Those SOCIAL types will have a great time and enjoy the team process, but, bottom line, the task would be better delegated to a well-balanced team. Put a driver on the team to make the decisions, an analytical to make sure they consider all the options and don't just jump to a conclusion, and suddenly the socializers and expressive team members will have direction. They are able to solicit the full participation of all members because they make working together fun while the others hold it together and keep them on task.

If you are delegating to an individual, there are some pitfalls to consider. Because it is the manger who is, again, ultimately responsible, some managers tend to delegate to the same person. They know that person will get the job done, and it will be completed with the same quality and attention they themselves would have shown, so they tend to overwork the same delegate. There are dangers of always delegating to the same person, though.

If you delegate to the same person, others on the team may feel as though you are playing favorites. If this feeling gets too strong, salespeople who are left out may seek challenges by changing to another company, or moving to another management team—especially if recognition is one of their stronger motivations.

Another danger of delegating to the same person is that they will suffer burnout because you have burdened them with too much responsibility, and they didn't know how to say "No." There is no time to reward that particular person, or time for them to celebrate because one task begins to run right into another. When this happens, the one being delegated to doesn't feel privileged any longer, but rather burdened with too much work and too little time.

Step #3:   Briefing
This can be one of the most difficult areas of delegating.

> If you delegate with too little information, the responsibility party has no clear direction. If you give too much information, you may stifle the creativity of those doing the work, or be perceived as though you are unwilling to give up control of the project.

During the briefing process, make sure you give your people opportunities to question, to investigate and to develop their own plan. Sometimes it's better to give them possible resources for problem solving and keep your opinions to yourself until they have processed the information and formed their own questions.

Remember, this step is called "defining the task" not controlling the task, or problem solving for the task. It takes all the challenge out of the project if you determine all the solutions. I once heard,

> "The worst kind of workers to have are the ones who do nothing that they are told, or the ones who do nothing MORE than they are told."

Allow your people to discover, plan, implement and follow through. When you do, you will be amazed at what can be accomplished.

Step #4:   Control

By this, I don't mean standing over the shoulder of those to whom you delegate and directing their performance. No! Instead, in the "control" phase of delegation, managers need to have in place some sort of monitoring system. You can monitor by reports, through activity sheets, or by meeting with team leaders who are responsible for delivering you the status of the project. Your job in this phase is to encourage your people. Let them know you are available to remove the obstacles to their achievement.

Once you have delegated—keep your distance. Easier said than done. It's easy to allow an individual or team to accomplish when they are on the ball and experiencing no stumbling blocks. The difficulty comes when you believe there is an easier, more efficient method, and you want to just take the project back or control the functioning of the group.

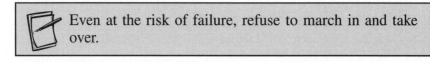

> Even at the risk of failure, refuse to march in and take over.

Guide your people. Coach them toward greater successes. Do what it takes to develop their skills rather than demand their submission.

Step #5:   Appraisal

This is the review and revise step. It can be performed after the project or task is complete, but it should be done together with your team or the individual you are reviewing. For longer projects, appraisals can be held at regularly planned intervals to monitor progress. You may find you need to revise expectations or deadlines. You may find you need to recruit another team member who's an expert in that area. Or, you may discover your people need the advice of outside people, and you need to adjust the budget in order to complete the project.

Be sure to keep records of outcomes and appraisals in order to use them again in similar situations. When you do, you will be better able to project more accurate deadlines, budgets and delegates when the next task of a similar nature comes to your attention. Experiences with successes and setbacks only serve to hone you and your team's skills.

The Cost of Avoiding Delegation

Delegation can come at a cost to the manger, but the cost of avoiding delegation can be even more devastating. If you refuse to delegate, your time limitations may cause so much disorganization that great opportunities slip through the cracks. You'll be too burned out to care about the development of your people, and they'll be frustrated at the absence of self-improvement or team growth.

> Managers who fail to delegate usually have poor performance because they miss deadlines or have routine processes slowed down to a crawl.

Their people aren't challenged or motivated to achieve, and they soon move on to a company or manager that allows them to achieve at their highest level.

What Is Holding You Back?

If you believe in delegating, why don't you do more of it? What is holding you back form becoming an effective delegator? It's what we talked about earlier—negative feelings of insecurity and mistrust. If you believe that you do it better than anybody else, you will never provide an opportunity to be proven wrong. I can guarantee you, your performance won't be better than everybody else's if you never have the time to complete your projects.

Some managers also fear delegating because they don't want to burden their people. I've found just the opposite to be true. People become better time managers when they have more to do. Have you ever noticed how much you can accomplish in a busy day? But, if you've given yourself all weekend to do a task that would only take an hour, you will postpone the task until you have little time to complete it. Through your procrastination you will have allowed it to worry you all weekend or forget to do it altogether.

> If you learn to delegate properly, your people won't feel burdened—they will appreciate the challenge and trust you have given them.

And, they'll enjoy the recognition they get from upper management when you give them all the credit for achievement. Before you can be an effective delegator, learn to deal with your own fears of delegating. One of the strongest fears managers have, yet the most difficult to admit, is the manager's fear that salespeople will out perform them. Possessive feelings about work are negative and unproductive. Let go of them. Be willing to lose some of the control, yet still accept ultimate responsibility.

Know this—fears are caused by your own insecurities. Once you are able to set aside those insecurities, you'll realize that delegation to top performers makes you and them look much more capable. Effective leaders have a clear desk because they concentrate on a small number of prioritized tasks and delegate everything else.

If either you or your salespeople lack trust, the delegation process falls short of the mark. Managers need to first show trust and belief in their salespeople. Then their salespeople will trust that they will be supported and given credit for their individual and team achievements.

Be A Considerate Delegator

Make those you delegate to feel safe about stepping out on a limb and pushing themselves to greater levels of performance. Be willing to catch them if they lose their balance, but allow them to discover the fun and adventure of completing the task.

Being considerate to your people also means not requiring them to participate or attend meetings on projects that are not relevant to their current projects and accounts. Or, if their expertise is only needed during one phase of the project, keep them informed about what is going on, but require their presence only during the phase that pertains to them. Their input may only be 10 percent of the entire team's effort. Of course, when rewarded for the accomplishments of the team, they will only be receiving 10 percent of the rewards. There is nothing more demotivating than to delegate unnecessary tasks. Who of us has the time to give to busy work? Not me! Not you, I'm sure. And, definitely not your people.

If possible, clear the delegations with your superiors. Let them know the purpose of your selections and how you plan to use the additional time this gives you to move forward in areas that would otherwise be neglected. This isn't always possible; sometimes your superiors don't care how the job gets done or by whom; they just want to know that it's being done.

Many time management issues must be addressed when considering delegation. Not only your time, but the time of those to whom you delegate. How many of you believe it is better to do the tough tasks first? Sorry to say, that might be getting you into trouble when you are prioritizing. The difficult tasks may not be what needs to be accomplished first. Prioritizing is really a sequential thing. Do what needs to be done first—first.

Prioritize Your Delegated Tasks

Don't do projects in order of seniority or by degree of difficulty first. The following are examples of some tasks that can be grouped:

- Administrative Duties Outside the Realm of Secretarial = Paperwork or reports for a project may be burdensome to a driver personality, but given to one who is analytical, and they are right in their element.
- Human Resources Duties = If you need to bring in an outside advisor, let your expressive personalities or socializers be responsible for interviewing them and finding that perfectly matched person for the team. They love working with people and will know what type has the individual skills and knowledge while still working well with the team.
- Financial Needs = Give these to your team's accountant or budget person. Let them figure out how to increase your dollars or expand your profit centers.

It is great to split tasks on a project because it allows you to work on several things at once. If you are delegating to an individual, be sure to provide the resources necessary to help them achieve success within the time frame you have agreed upon.

Another way to prioritize is to make a "to do" list. Draw up a delegation plan. Inform your salespeople of the plan well in advance. Make sure your delegates know who to report to, and then provide supportive coaching. Lastly, monitor their progress and be there to help them when they encounter what they believe to be insurmountable hurdles. Other than that—get out of the way and let them do the work you've entrusted them to do.

The following is a sample delegation checklist or form that will help you with each delegated task.

DELEGATION FORM

Describe the Task

_____

_____

Name the Delegate   **Completion Date**

_____   _____

Anticipated Challenges

_____

_____

_____

Outside/Inside Resources

_____

_____

_____

Expectations/Method of Measurement

_____

_____

_____

When delegating, it's a good idea to also let the delegate give you his or her time frame, complete with possible conflicts and completion obstacles. You may even want to set a completion time range rather than one date. In other words, in a perfect world, you would like the task to be completed on or before this date, but your drop-dead time frame is really on this date. After the entire project has been completed, give delegates an opportunity to self-evaluate. Ask them what they could have done to increase performance and what changes they plan to make on their next delegation. Let them know you appreciate their work, and show your appreciation by offering payment, praise and recognition for a job well done.

Delegate—Then Get Out of the Way of Your People

Salespeople who are continuously training and conditioning will create constant, never-ending improvement. They won't always need your supervision. Sometimes the process that needs the most improvement isn't the one your people are going through, but rather the process of learning how to delegate that you yourself are experiencing. Here's how you can step out of the way of your people and minimize the risk of failure:

1. Anticipate problems before they prevent ongoing production.
2. Have "Plan B" ready in case the unexpected happens—it most usually does.
3. If you have made a mistake in delegating, remove him or her from the project or partner the salesperson with another who can help the team reach its highest potential.
4. Accept new ideas and allow outside sources in if necessary.
5. Be careful about offering too much help; it can be perceived as interference.

Praise & Reward

The last step to effective delegation, but perhaps the most important, is the praise and reward. Thank your team for their efforts.

When things go wrong—look for solutions not scapegoats.

When things go well, recognize all the great things they accomplished. Be a believer in second chances and you will be celebrating far more successes when you delegate.

Working Through the Process--Chapter Eleven

❖ How do you currently delegate tasks? What are the strengths and weaknesses of your delegation methods?

Current Methods of Delegation:

_____

_____

Strengths:

_____

_____

Weaknesses:

_____

_____

❖ What is it costing you to continue practicing the same methods of delegation, or to avoid delegating altogether?

_____

_____

_____

❖ What holds you back from practicing effective delegation?

_____

_____

_____

❖ List at least five tasks you are doing now that could easily be delegated.

1. _____

2. _____

3. _____

4. _____

5. _____

❖ How would you be a more satisfied and effective manager by delegating the tasks listed above?

_____

_____

_____

❖ Plan to delegate and then get out of the way of your people and let them achieve!

1. If your salespeople are _____ _____, they won't need your constant _____.

2. Every _____ can be _____--even your own!

3. Determine the _____ of delegating.

4. Minimize the risks by...

   • _____ problems.
   • Establishing a "Plan B" for those _____ occurrences.
   • Creating delegation _____ with your people.
   • _____ new ideas and _____ outside sources in if necessary.
   • Refusing to _____ with the _____ of your people.

❖ What methods will you use to praise and reward new delegates?

_____

_____

CHAPTER TWELVE

**Let's Get to the "MEET" of the Matter
(Managing Effective Sales Meetings)**

 "Spectacular achievement is always preceded by spectacular preparation."
Dr. Robert Schuller

Chapter Highlights:

▶ Conducting Your BEST Sales Meetings
▶ Facilitating vs. Leading the Sales Meeting
▶ Types of Meetings
▶ Meeting Methods
▶ Meeting Plan and Agenda
▶ Sample Meeting Form
▶ Making it Memorable and FUN!

Meetings make up a big percentage of most managers' days. The average 45-year-old manager will have spent approximately 17,000 hours in business meetings within a 20-year period. In many companies, more money is spent on meetings than on any other aspect of their business. Obviously, somebody believes it is important to hold meetings. What about you? Do you often question why you are having this meeting, anyway? Well, let's take a look at that.

Although not the case with every meeting, effective sales meetings should be a more efficient method of producing positive results. Few salespeople oppose meetings if they are relevant and productive. It's when their superiors expect a meeting to be the end-all to everything that the salespeople balk. In actuality, meetings are really where the action first begins and the wheels of change start to roll forward.

Meetings that Matter

One of the most productive things you can do as a manager is to promise not to hold meetings that do nothing more than spend your salespeople's time and your company's money. In fact, that's the purpose of this chapter—to teach you how to make a plan for your sales meetings that encourage attendees to actively participate.

Meetings should offer you high returns on your company's investment of time and money. One of the worst things your salespeople can experience is to walk away from a meeting wondering what was accomplished—feeling like they could have had a more productive time returning calls and completing paperwork.

Unfortunately, not every meeting is effective and efficient. There can be hidden explosives in the agenda that make your salespeople feel as though they are walking into a mine field where each step must be tested and the progress is slow going. How can you defuse these mines? Well, first you have to recognize they exist.

Twelve Tanks that Can Overpower the Mines of Your Best Sales Meetings

1. <u>Be A Fearless Leader</u>
   If you do not establish control of your sales meetings, it doesn't take long for them to get chaotic. For example, determine what will be discussed and who will be responsible for special presentations. There should be an understood protocol in even the most informal meetings.

> Don't let one person dominate the conversation and others sleep in the back of the room. It's your sales meeting—you are responsible to make sure it works.

2. <u>Be Prompt and Encourage that Behavior in Others</u>
   How can a manager who is consistently 10-15 minutes late expect his or her salespeople to be on time? This is one of the teachable

moments when your people learn best by your example. So, if the meeting is to be held at 9:00 a.m., start at 9:00 a.m. sharp.

> It helps to hold routine sales meetings on the same day at the same time each week or month.

It is also wise to plan consecutive topics that are given to the salespeople a month in advance so they know how one topic covered in a sales meeting is related to the following one.

3. <u>End Your Meetings On Time</u>
    If the meeting goes on forever, your people will become bored and tune out the good with the boring. Keep their interest.

> Vary the format. Bring in guest speakers or special information that will draw them into the meeting topics or discussions.

4. <u>Boredom is an Attendance Killer</u>
    Some of your salespeople will think of any excuse not to attend one of your meetings. Instead of blaming them for their lack of interest, why not look to yourself for solutions. How can you make your sales meetings more interesting—more imaginative? I know it can be difficult to be creative and innovative when you are up to your eyeballs in work. All you want to do is get through the sales meeting and get on with things. If this is the case, I encourage you to start looking at your sales meetings with a different perspective. Look at them as a time to inspire your people. Look at them as a time to develop strong bonds as a team. Look at them as a time to reward, praise and recognize outstanding performances. I can guarantee you, your salespeople won't hesitate to attend one of your sales meetings when they know there is something valuable in it for them.

5. <u>Everybody May be Working from Their Own Private Agendas</u>
    It is up to you as a leader to determine what will be discussed and decided upon in the meeting. Make sure to plan an agenda and communicate that agenda to all your salespeople. If you have time, you might want to ask for their input on additional agenda items prior to the meeting.

> Get your people in the habit of thinking "If it's NOT on the agenda—it's NOT going to be discussed."

That may sound strict and unbending, but drastic times call for drastic measures. If you have already created a situation where your sales meetings are out of control and nothing gets accomplished, you may have to be very rigid about your agendas in the beginning. Down the road, you can loosen up, but make your agendas your meetings' map for success.

6. The Leaders May Have Unrealistic Expectations

Managers often expect full cooperation when they haven't done much to encourage ownership in the process or outcome of the meeting. At the time, salespeople may expect to be entertained, have their own private challenges discussed, then selfishly step out when they have had their individual needs met.

Meetings are about the group. They should address challenges and objectives of the team, not the individual, unless, of course, it's a one-on-one meeting about that particular individual's sales challenges or progress.

> Individual needs and issues should be reserved for personal reviews or private meetings with management.

7. You and Your People May Have too Many Distractions

Your top producer may be looking forward to closing that big account and be expecting a call from the customer at any moment. Consequently, that top salesperson will be looking at his or her watch and doing a mental countdown. Your newcomer might be worried that this is cutting into his or her prospecting time. And, as manager, you may be distracted with how you will ever get the quarterly reports out on time if you can never stop attending meetings.

No matter how difficult, try to stay one-minded in your sales meetings. Your focus should be on helping to develop your people and on coaching them in new strategies and skills. If the distractions stand in the way of the success of your sales meetings, then you should be considering a different location. Get yourself and your people outside the normal work environment. That in itself might give them something to look forward to.

> While eliminating much of the normal office distractions, changing locations can also stimulate creative thought and enthusiasm on the part of your salespeople.

8. Lack of Communication
    If you haven't clearly communicated the change of location to your salespeople, you are going to have them strolling in 10-15 minutes late. Sometimes the clearest message communicated is that you have failed to establish a definite direction and effective plan. If that continues, you will have NO attendees. Plan your sales meetings. Choose different topics relevant to your salespeople's needs. Use different resources in your presentations. Have different people contribute. Invite outside sources to come speak in your sales meetings. Give your meetings direction. Be a leader!

9. Too Many People in One Meeting
    If you have a large team, you may want to consider two meetings each week or month and split the groups. Or, if your sales meeting pertains to a particular topic, some of your salespeople who are not having difficulties in that area may not need to attend. Let them use each moment to its fullest and most productive.

> In fact, I have found the best sales meetings are those in which the manager was clever enough to make attending a prestigious thing.

It was a privilege to be invited to attend the meeting.

10. Poor Attitudes and Dissatisfied Salespeople
    These people can make a sales meeting an uncomfortable experience for everybody. If something needs to be cleared or aired before the meeting, do it. If there is an overall, prevailing attitude of discontent, perhaps that should be your sales meeting topic.

11. Unclear Objectives and Agendas

These can also cause some sales meeting challenges. If your people don't know why they are expected to meet, they either walk into the sales meeting unprepared, or they question whether it is necessary for them to be there at all. Agendas with a meeting objective will give your salespeople time to mull over what you will be discussing and to consider how they feel about the topic.

> If you enjoy a more interactive meeting, be sure to give them the agenda and meeting objectives.

12. So Little Time to Plan a Sales Meeting

The more planned the meeting the more successful the outcome. Most of the time, sales meetings seem more like a gathering of "What did you do this week?" than a productive time to decide, plan implementation methods, and commit to success. If your time is so rushed that you cannot plan effectively for every sales meeting, why not delegate some of the meetings to your top salespeople. Let them take a meeting and present a topic that they consider their strength.

Is it a manager's responsibility to plan and lead every sales meeting? Absolutely not! In fact, it's more interesting to hear other's perspectives on the subject.

> Whether you are leading the meeting or participating in the meeting, every person has a part and each part is integral to the meeting's overall success.

Let's talk about some of the roles of those attending your sales meetings.

Who's Doing What?

One of the most difficult roles is the facilitator's. As a facilitator, it is your job to remain neutral. This is not easy when you have ownership in the topic—when you are emotionally involved or passionately interested. As a facilitator, it is your job to direct the process not the conversation. Sometimes the facilitator acts like the meeting police—managing emotionally charged situations.

> The primary job of the facilitator is to provide feedback and keep the sales meeting moving forward.

Not to be confused with the facilitator, the LEADER of the sales meeting is most responsible for the effectiveness of the meeting.

> It is up to the leader to define the meeting objective, select the participants, decide on the meeting's location and confirm the time the meeting will be held.

If your sales meetings are always held at the same time each week or month, a reminder may still be necessary.

It's up to the leader to prepare the agenda as well. A good idea when preparing the agenda is to have the participation from your salespeople before the meeting. Send them a preliminary agenda and ask for their input, then include some of their suggestions. The more participation you can give them in the agenda, the more you get in the meeting.

Next, we have the meeting recorder.

> Recorders are the eyes and ears of the meeting—the meeting's memory.

They may choose to tape the meeting and transcribe the tape to make sure they miss nothing. It's the recorder's job is to notify everyone of what took place in the meeting. It also serves as a reminder to those who may have special responsibilities decided upon in the meeting. The recorder verifies all the decisions that were made.

The timekeeper's job doesn't sound all that important, but it is definitely needed. Timekeepers not only keep the time during the entire meeting, but they let others know the time spent on each agenda item.

> If you have a good timekeeper, he or she should not allow you to spend all the meeting time on just one or two items.

A good thing to do in order to help the timekeeper and the team evenly spread out their time between agenda items is to put suggested time frames on each issue.

Lastly, we have the participants. Participants must be well prepared. The more informed they are on the topics, the better the results of the meeting.

> Suggest that attendees come with a list of questions, or with example scenarios in mind that can be discussed in the meeting.

Make sure the leader has materials ready for the participants. When necessary, those materials should be distributed ahead of time for their review.

Types of Meetings

We've talked about the roles of those attending your sales meetings—now let's talk about the types of meetings you can hold.

- Routine Sales Meetings
  These are mostly concerned with the process of something. Most sales meetings would fall into this category, along with staff meetings, project updates and committee meetings.

- Occasional Emergency Sales Meetings
  These are held separately from the weekly or monthly meetings. Perhaps your company is rolling out a new product or your team has a certain problem that needs to be resolved. These meetings are the exception to the rule because they have a short-term mission and usually little time for careful planning. However, if your people have been educated about meeting protocol, those good habits will spill over even when the urgency of the meeting demands a spur-of-the-moment gathering.

  Emergency meetings should be conducted by a leader who has a clear picture of the urgent situation. It could be one of your salespeople or an outside advisor. No matter who leads the meeting, keep these meetings small in numbers and short in time.

> Above all, make sure there IS an emergency when you call an urgent meeting.

If you cry "wolf" too many times, soon your salespeople will stop believing in your emergencies and just keep "tending" to sales while your emergency meeting takes place.

- Informational Sharing Meetings
  These types of meetings are held to gain or give information quickly to a large group at one time. When it comes to sales meetings, they are more informational when it is a regional or divisional sales meeting that delivers new information about the company or a company update. It's also an excellent way to have informational sales meetings with other departments to see the results of what you did last quarter and how those things affected customer service or the engineers in product development—if you work in a manufacturing organization.

- Problem-Solving Meetings
  This type of meeting focuses on a problem and identifies SEVERAL solutions or possible alternative resolutions to the problem. The word SEVERAL is key here to this type of meeting.

 When possible, give your salespeople the choice of what solution works best for them.

- Decision-Making Meetings
  These are a common type of meeting for salespeople, and they usually stem from problem-solving meetings. Out of the several alternative solutions, the salespeople may be asked to review what works best for them then come together in a decision-making meeting to arrive at a consensus about which solution to implement.

- Planning Meetings
  These types of meetings follow the progress of newly implemented decisions. In these, strategies are adopted and deadlines are set. Many times, in planning meetings, delegation of tasks occurs too. Before these meetings are over . . .

  1. Make sure the delegate understands what is to be done and has the capabilities to do it.

2. Ask yourself if you have addressed a proper time frame or completion date.
3. Check to see if your team has been given the authority to function efficiently.
4. Double check to see if you have put the proper checkpoints in place to monitor the team's progress.

• Evaluation Meetings
These are made up of the people who are the guardians for the project.

> It is their job to evaluate the team's progress and trouble shoot areas of concern.

They are also used for planning the celebrations for your team's successes and the examination of their setbacks.

• Type-combination Meetings
These are most common when you have a smaller sales team that must wear several hats. Then, you can combine the functions of several meetings into one. For example, the purpose of one meeting might be to gather information, problem solve, delegate and develop a plan of action—all in the same meeting.

Meeting Methods

The meeting types address the "WHAT"—the meeting methods look at the "HOW." So, let's examine the HOW or meeting methods that could be used by you and your salespeople.

• Guided Discussion
This is the most common method used. The chairperson or leader conducts the meeting sitting at the table head and the agenda is strictly followed.

• Round-Robin Meeting Method
This discussion style makes for a highly interactive group. It's commonly used when there will be reporting from many people on your sales team.

- Brainstorming Method
It is a structured, very verbal, solution-seeking meeting method. Brainstorming meetings are marked by levels of creativity and spontaneity. Because this method requires your salespeople to share innovative ideas, the team leader should commit to creating a "no blame" atmosphere.

> It's up to you to set the stage for positive attitudes and acceptance of every idea.

Not that you'll use every idea, but even the most outlandish should be heard. Who knows, modify those seemingly "off the wall" ideas, and they can make great innovations to your sales team. It's also important to keep these meetings short—perhaps only 20-25 minutes.

- One-on-One Sales Meeting Method
One-on-one does constitute a meeting. In this meeting method, an individual's specific challenges or strengths can be better discussed. You can look to see how specific behaviors, habits and beliefs are affecting that particular salesperson's sales results. This may also be the time to hash out personal problems the salesperson is having with a peer, or a family member outside the workplace that might be adversely affecting his or her performance.

> Believe it or not, your people are much more likely to let their personal lives spill over into the workplace than allow their work lives to spill over into their personal lives.

Keep in mind, although it is one of the most effective types of meetings, it certainly isn't the most efficient. It usually involves a manager and one or two salespeople.

- The Progress Interview Meeting Method
It too is a one-on-one, but most of the time there is only the manager and one salesperson involved. It needs to be well planned with a clearly communicated objective. If you want a lot of interaction between yourself and your salesperson, make it more informal and open.

- The Hit and Run Meeting Method
  It is deliberate and highly focused—quick and to the point. The thing to look out for in this meeting method is that the others don't feel like you are taking advantage of their time. These meetings should be infrequent and very specific, involving only those who need to attend.

The Meeting Plan and Agenda

If you only learn one thing about meetings in this chapter, it should be this next sentence.

 Know when to hold 'em—know when to fold 'em!

Avoid holding unnecessary meetings, and NEVER let yourself be known as the ENDLESS meeting facilitator. I've mentioned the meeting plan and agenda several times, but they aren't always the easiest to do, especially when you are pressed for time, which is all the time, right? Planning and creating a working agenda is the most needed yet the most neglected part of any meeting.

Getting everything you've been thinking about in your head into the meeting format is difficult to do without a plan and an agenda. Here's what to consider when planning your agenda:

1. Why is the meeting being held?
2. What are your expectations?
3. Who is needed to do what? (role definition)
4. Where is the meeting being held?
5. When will you start and end the meeting?

One of the easiest ways to plan a meeting and create an agenda is to have a form that might include the following:

Sample Meeting Form

Date of Meeting: _____   **Time:** _____

Location: _____

Meeting Topic: _____

Meeting Purpose: _____
                       _____
                       _____

Discussion Items: _____
                       _____
                       _____

Desired Results: _____
                       _____
                       _____

Method/Type: _____

List of Attendees: _____
                       _____
                       _____
                       _____

Aids/Equipment: _____

Facilitator: _____

Meeting Costs: _____

Prepare—Prepare—Prepare

Once you get this down, gather all your meeting materials and equipment.

> Make sure your meeting format will appeal to the visual learners as well as the auditory learners.

You may consider providing presentation materials in the form of handouts, or you may want to show slides or use overhead transparencies. If you use any electronic equipment, make sure all your equipment is in good working order—and so are you. In other words, be familiar with how to operate the equipment you plan to use in your meeting. Nothing will make you feel more inadequate than standing before those you lead and being dysfunctional on a simple little piece of equipment. Take a few moments before the meeting to check out all your equipment and line up your materials. When making comparisons, make sure that you offer visual graphics or artistic comparisons. It drives your point home and makes your meetings much more memorable.

The Fruits of Your Labor

It's really quite rewarding when you see the fruits of your labor—when your people go out into the field and implement what was discussed in the meeting. Give credit to your team for its efforts. Recognize those who successfully planned, implemented and trouble shot your meeting. Follow up on the project's progress and keep both attendees and upper management informed as to the progress. Reward a successful team and some of its individual members for special efforts. And, if all goes well, be sure to congratulate yourself for being a great facilitator.

Speaking of memorable—HAVE FUN!

> You will be surprised at how much more you will accomplish and how few challenges you will have in your meetings if you make them fun.

Make it a point in your planning stage to incorporate something surprising, something that your people will get a kick out of doing. When you do, your people won't have a problem attending and participating in your meetings. How you hold your meetings will be carried out into your project groups. If you have a great time in the meeting, they will be excited and eager to continue that attitude. Give your people a great start by being a GREAT meeting facilitator.

Working Through the Process--Chapter Twelve

❖ List at least five things that commonly go wrong in your sales meetings?

1. _____

2. _____

3. _____

4. _____

5. _____

❖ What could be done to eliminate the above problems?

_____

_____

_____

❖ Twelve Most Common Problems Inhibiting the Effectiveness of Today's Sales Meetings.

1. Leader cannot _____ and the meeting lacks _____.
2. People arrive _____.
3. Meeting _____ too _____.
4. The meeting is _____ and attendees get _____.
5. No _____ and the meeting gets _____ on _____ issues.
6. People don't feel _____ and managers expect full _____.
7. Too many _____.
8. No meeting _____ or specific _____.
9. Too many _____.
10. Poor _____ due to mandated attendance.
11. Unclear _____ and/or _____.
12. No time given for _____ information.

❖ Types of Meetings

1. _____ Meetings, such as _____, _____ and _____ meetings.
2. _____ Meetings designed to produce a _____ or _____.
3. _____ _____ Meeting to _____ or _____ information quickly.
4. _____ Meeting--focused on the _____ to discover possible _____ solutions.
5. _____ Meeting usually stems from the _____ _____ meeting.
6. _____ Meeting that _____ the decisions.
7. _____ Meeting held to _____ _____ and _____ _____.
8. _____ Meeting that contain _____ meeting types in one.

❖ How can you vary the types of sales meetings you have? What will those changes mean to your sales meetings?

Types of Sales Meetings You Commonly Hold:

_____

_____

_____

How Do You Plan to Create a Variety?

_____

_____

_____

❖ List at least three things in each category that you plan to do differently in your next sales meeting.

Preparation:

1. _____

2. _____

3. _____

Presentation:

1. _____

2. _____

3. _____

Follow-up:

1. _____

2. _____

3. _____

❖ Things to consider when planning a meeting.

1. _____ of the meeting.
2. Meeting _____ or _____.
3. Meeting _____ or _____.
4. Desired _____ of the meeting.
5. Proper and most _____ meeting _____.
6. _____ time most convenient to all parties.
7. _____ time you expect each member to adhere to.
8. _____ to the company and expected _____ on their investment.
9. _____ or _____ of meeting.
10. Who will be _____ to _____?
11. _____ each member will play in the meeting.
12. _____ to be discussed in the meeting.

❖ How do you plan on making your sales meetings memorable and FUN?

_____

_____

_____

_____

CHAPTER THIRTEEN
Communicating Clearly

 "Courage is what it takes to stand up and <u>speak</u>; courage is also what it takes to sit down and <u>listen</u>."
Winston S. Churchill

Chapter Highlights:

▶ Practicing Better Basics
▶ Increasing Your Sales Knowledge
▶ Barriers to Effective Communications
▶ Body Language (Between the Lines Communication)
▶ Investigative Communicating for Results

The more knowledge your people have, the better able they will be to implement that knowledge in the field. The better they are able to share their knowledge and combine it with sound selling skills, the more success they will enjoy in their careers. All this is made possible through clear and thorough communications. Before we go into some special communicating scenarios and remedies, I wanted to review with you what your salespeople will need to know to feel confident and achieve greater success.

> Ask yourself what you and your company are currently doing to help increase the level of expertise and professionalism of your people.

We know you are continuously learning and preparing to be outstanding at knowing how to develop your people, and that's why you're reading this book. But let's look at some of the fundamentals you'll need to make sure you communicate to your people. How will you prepare them for excellence in selling?

Most managers came up through the ranks of salespeople and were promoted because of their outstanding selling skills. So, it may seem strange to be reviewing the basics. You may even assume that your people are all familiar with the fundamentals as well. Here's what I have discovered, though, through my workshops and seminars.

> The <u>basics</u> are our bread and butter in sales, and we've got more people in sales who are starving because they don't practice basic selling principles.

The more your salespeople know about the fundamentals, the more ownership they will have in the entire sales team and the company. Keeping this in mind, let's review some of those sales fundamentals. While we do, I want you to think of how you are making sure your salespeople know this information and are applying it in selling situations.

Back to Better Basics

Most companies don't have trouble with the first fundamental, and that is to give their salespeople knowledge of the company. That's a gimmee! What I have found is that the knowledge isn't thorough enough. It usually just centers on what is happening now, instead of where your company came from—its roots. Here is a list of questions your salespeople should not only be able to answer, but should know how to link the information to buyer benefits.

About the Company
1. <u>How did your company begin in the business</u>?
    Knowing a short history of your company will help to give you and your company credibility, especially if your company has been around a long time. If your company is a newcomer to the industry, you'll need to know where the founders of your company received their expertise.

2. <u>How long have they been providing these products and services to the marketplace</u>?
Again, this is a good credibility builder. Customers want to know your company is going to be around at least for as long as they will need your product and/or service. If you are presenting a new product or service to a customer, make sure they understand that this product was developed from your company's response to the needs of their many customers. Let them know that while it might be a new product or service, it certainly isn't a new company.

3. <u>What is the success rate of your company</u>?
I would feel safe to say that many of your salespeople don't know this about your company. They may have some vague idea of what position your company holds in the marketplace, but they don't have statistical information that they can share with their customers about the success rate of your company. Make sure that you provide them with that information, then verify that they are using the information you're offering.

4. <u>What are their current products and services</u>?
This may sound so easy if yours is a company with few products and services, but some manufacturing operations may have hundreds of products available. What happens is that salespeople will get comfortable selling only a handful of those products and then miss opportunities to create greater opportunities because they are unfamiliar with all the products and services of your company.

5. <u>What is their vision for the company</u>?
Over and over again, I find that leaders with small vision usually recruit salespeople with small vision. So, I would encourage you, if you don't know it now, to investigate the true vision of your company. What is your company's picture of future success? Then ask yourself how your company's vision aligns with your own vision for your career. After you've taken the time to analyze these things for yourself, it's time to encourage your salespeople to do the same. It will soon become apparent whose vision needs to be expanded.

Help your people broaden their vision. How? Share your vision with them.

Have your top producers do the same. Let them see that the picture you have of your company is directly related to the way you sell your company's products and services. Bigger picture—greater sales!

6. What do these future plans mean to customers?
Once they've broadened their vision, teach them how to share this picture with their customers. Your customers will want to know how doing business with a company of your stature and vision will personally benefit them—and it's up to your salespeople to deliver that message. That's what helps to differentiate your company from all the others offering similar products and services.

About the Product

This leads us right into the next piece of knowledge you'll need to make sure all your people know—they'll need to know the product and how its ownership will benefit their customers. How are your products made? What warranties do they have? What do other customers think of your products and services? Are there any different uses they've communicated to you that could be passed on to your people? That last question is a very important one, and one that few of your salespeople are taking full advantage of. Let your loyal customers help your salespeople sell their product. Because they have worked with your products for a long time, they may have developed some unique uses for that product. Knowing just how they are enjoying your product or service will help you to pass on valuable information that might help another prospective customer to make up their mind to own. So, encourage your salespeople to keep in contact with their customers and discover the various ways they are putting your products and services to work for their companies.

About the Customer

The next component of knowledge for your salespeople is to KNOW YOUR CUSTOMERS! Knowing the answers to the following questions can double and triple their sales.

1. Who is their customer?
There is nothing worse than your salespeople investing precious time and money on prospects that won't benefit from your product and have

no real use of your services. If your salespeople don't know their customers, not only will it be difficult to make that first sale, but forget being able to take advantage of possible upgrades and add-ons. I guarantee you, if they haven't stopped to ask themselves how your company's products and services can serve the needs of this particular customer before the meeting, the customer will ask it during the meeting. I've seen this one simple question completely take a salesperson by surprise who didn't stop to discover if this person was one who could benefit from owning your products and services.

2. <u>Where do they find new leads</u>?
Are you coaching your people on where to find new leads? Do you encourage them to get referrals, to work your files and find past customers who for one reason or another have stopped using your products and services? Do you brainstorm ways to find new leads? Finding new leads doesn't necessarily mean that your salespeople have to get all that creative.

New leads can be found in old places, you know.

One way to discover ways to generate new leads is to have all your people list five favorite prospecting ideas and then share them with the group. Let your salespeople learn from one another. Take all these lists and keep a leads generation file that can be shared with every new recruit.

3. <u>When, how and why do the customers buy</u>?
Every product and service has a selling cycle. That cycle indicates to your salespeople when they should be returning to their customers for another order or an upgraded product. It's not only important to understand when your customers will be buying, but what moves them to own your product. What moves one customer may be quite different from what motivates another. That's why your salespeople need to develop long-lasting relationships with their customers so they know how and why they make their buying decisions. Some buy because they want to help their people do their jobs easier. Others buy your

product or service because this decision will make them look good to their superiors. No matter what their motivation, your salespeople need to know how to appeal to their customers' individual needs.

> Most of all, encourage your people to LISTEN more than they TALK – to become the investigator and discover exactly what their customer needs.

4. <u>How do the customers benefit from each of your offerings</u>?
    Often times, customers have their budgets in mind when they are ready to make a buying decision. It's up to you to teach your people that they need to change the perspective of their customers. Help them to focus on the benefits of ownership—the value of your product and service—rather than keeping their eye on the price.

> There is a big difference between price and value. Price is set and so is your customer's budget! Value is created—and that's exactly what your salespeople should be doing—creating value in your products and services in order to increase sales.

Once they've created value in one area, it's only natural for that customer to turn to the salespeople they already know and feel comfortable with for future needs.

About the Competitor

The next one is where many of your people fail to do their homework—KNOW YOUR COMPETITION! Keep informed of your competition, and pass on the information to your salespeople. Who are your people competing against, and what is your competitor's success ratio? One of the things many managers have found to be a valuable tool is the Comparison Matrix. A Comparison Matrix offers a visual to your salespeople who are visual learners. The Matrix lets them visualize and better represent their products and services to the customers.

Review with your salespeople the strengths and weaknesses of the comparisons made on that Matrix. Then go over with your people how to address those things in their sales presentations.

> Teach them how to turn an objection into an advantage—how to tackle, head on, what might be perceived as a weakness in your product or service, and then change that perception in the eyes of their customers.

About their Particular Job Requirements

Lastly, give your salespeople a clear understanding about their job responsibilities. Good managers clearly communicate answers to the following questions:

- How do they fill out the forms?
- How do they process the orders?
- What is expected of them as far as follow-up?
- What are the reporting requirements? When?
- What are your expectations? Have they been clearly communicated?
- What resources are available?
- Where do they get business cards and marketing materials, like brochures or newsletters?
- What about expense allowances and reports?
- Do your salespeople have mentors, or who can they go to with questions before coming to you?

It's been my experience that very few companies do more than simple product knowledge. About 70 percent of today's salespeople have had absolutely NO training. What about your people? Are they hungry to learn? That hunger is the way you, as a manager, can gage if you have the makings of a top producer. That's right! What do your top producers want to learn when most people think they know it all? It's your responsibility to make sure your people maintain an attitude of ongoing learning in order to master the art of selling!

Never Assume Your Salespeople Know

I'm sure you've heard that saying,

"To earn more you must learn more!"

So, stop assuming your salespeople know everything and start reinforcing the basics and introducing new and exciting selling strategies. Here are five points of interest for you to keep in mind when developing your salespeople.

1. Keep them challenged and interested with new and updated information.
2. Offer written materials that substantiate their verbal presentations.
3. The best managers share information and encourage their salespeople to do the same. They give them responsibilities in the sales meetings, in project groups and on special task forces.
4. The stream of communications should flow in both directions and never run dry. That's how you keep people interested and give them ownership in the company and your team.
5. Interested and challenged salespeople make better numbers, which makes their managers look great. It's to your advantage to take the time to communicate consistent, relevant and accurate information.

Train to Gain

So how is all this done? Through TRAINING! Excellent managers provide excellent training for their people. Build a foundation of strong fundamentals, then encourage them to learn from the best. There are many different kinds of training. Vary your educational offerings, such as:

- Seminars
- Workshops
- Mentorship Programs
- Audio/Video CD Libraries
- Books
- Role Playing Exercises
- Internet...and so much more

Just to name a few!

Communicate to Clients

Although most of us think primarily of presentations and speeches when we think of communications, effective communications includes more than just the spoken word. When it comes to communications, the responsibilities of a manager are incredible. I've seen many potentially great salespeople defeated because their communications skills were poor and their manager didn't know how or wasn't willing to help them develop better communication skills.

Why is all this left to managers? Sad to say, it's because the education system falls short of the mark in teaching our young people to effectively communicate. The written part of communications is what comprises the majority of communications studied in school. However the written word is not the major form of communications in the workplace.

What is? The spoken word—the sales presentation. Yet, we get very little education in speech. Unless your salespeople were on the debate team or took special speech classes in school, their training in speech may be next to nothing. I've found that many salespeople and managers alike find it helpful to join Toastmasters or other similar professional organizations in order to increase their comfort level when speaking to groups.

The last forms of communication are listening and observing. What kind of educational background would you say your salespeople have experienced before coming to work at your company? In most cases, practical experience in observation and listening has been their teacher. There is almost no formal education in these areas, and yet they are two of the most important components to effective communications.

Most of us are listening disabled by the time we graduate from college and seek our first positions in the marketplace.

Barriers to Effective Communication

1. <u>It is often difficult to establish a relationship with all your salespeople</u>. You may have been promoted into the department, and there are salespeople you, frankly, just don't care for. As manager, this can be difficult when it comes to doing your job well—which is to develop your people. Make up your mind to refuse to let personal feelings get in the way of your ability to effectively communicate.

2. <u>You don't agree with the opinions or suggestions being offered</u>.
    That's when you need to let your communications SKILLS override your

desire. Listen to your people and reserve judgment until you've heard what they have to say. If you're in a meeting, hold your tongue—let others comment first so that you won't unduly influence their communications.

3. <u>You just aren't interested in the topic being discussed, or you feel it's irrelevant to what needs to be discussed</u>.
Listen for a while, then lead the conversation back to the purpose of why you are communicating. Be patient though; you'd be surprised at what you can learn when you let someone ramble on a bit.

4. <u>There are external and internal distractions that are clouding your ability to deliver or receive information</u>.
It could be physical movement, noise, or maybe you're preoccupied with your own thoughts. When this happens, get up if you can. Change your position! Get a drink of water or go to the restroom. Do what is necessary to interrupt the distraction and clear your head.

5. <u>FEAR</u>
Fear is responsible for a lot of communication problems. Your salespeople may not communicate with you or their customers well because they are afraid of what you might say, or what the other person might think of what you say. You can tell when this is the case, both through their nonverbal language and by the rhythm and volume of their speech. Suddenly, your salespeople's speech might become slower and hesitant. When this happens, make them feel as comfortable as possible and their communication skills will rush to their rescue.

6. <u>Prejudging what your salespeople are talking about, and thinking you know what they are about to say so you offer the information for them</u>.
The longer your relationship with a salesperson, the more adept you are at the "you start—I'll finish" routine of communications. Avoid doing this; it may inhibit what they were truly meaning to communicate.

Overcoming the Barriers

With all these barriers in mind, how do you as a manager overcome them? The following are Five Tips to Overcoming Communication Barriers:

1. Find good in all your salespeople. Think of the advantages of having that particular salesperson on your team. Focus on their positive contributions to your team.
2. Remember; you don't have to agree. As a manager, it is often your job to play the devil's advocate. You don't have to agree, but you do need to listen. Stop focusing on YOUR feelings and start listening to THEIRS. The more tolerance you show, the more your salespeople will extend that same courtesy to you.
3. As manager, it's your responsibility to keep your people focused on the goals and objectives of the team. If the communications with a particular salesperson could be rough for him or her to hear because it is of a private nature, don't air it in public.
4. Hold important meetings or conferences in locations where you and your salespeople are least likely to be interrupted.
5. Active listening will help your salespeople get over their fear of rejection or disapproval. Let them see that you are listening. Shake your head. Give them a little "really" or "uh huh," now and then.

Communicating Between the Lines (body language)

What about the "between the line" communications? Those are buying signs that your salespeople need to be aware of so they can read between the lines when communicating with their customers.

I'll share a funny story with you. My parents could write the book on buying signs when car shopping. Because my dad doesn't want to let the salesperson know how they feel about a particular car, he always warns my mom before they get to the dealership to keep quiet when she sees one she really likes. Instead of telling dad she loves the car, they have this little communication system that goes on as they're looking. Dad does the investigating—you know the professional stuff like kicking the tires and looking under the hood. Mom handles the nonverbal communications like lifting her eyebrows in excitement, covering her mouth only to have a few enthusiastic squeaks escape, and giggling when she likes a car. Talk about "between the line" communications! Little do they know these buying signs speak louder and more effectively than any words.

Those nonverbal communications can be far more powerful than words. Why?

Nonverbal communications indicate the heart of your customer, where words can have double meanings or hidden messages.

Remember, as a manager your customers are your salespeople.

Something else to remember when reading your salespeople's nonverbal language—while you are reading customers or salespeople's body language, they are also reading yours.

Keep in mind, though, that these signs are not always reliable. Not 100 percent of the people who look down or hang their heads are hiding something or shy. It could be that they simply feel something crawling on their leg. Practice good judgment when reading the body language of others. Combine active listening with good questioning techniques. I'll talk about those questioning techniques in a minute.

Keys to Communicating for Results

1. Avoid playing favorites; make everyone feel important and valued.
2. Be visible to your people; visit them at their work sites.
3. Set aside time for one-on-ones.
4. Remember; honest disagreement can be fruitful.
5. Make your purpose known for meetings and conferences; hidden agendas can arouse suspicion.
6. Address false rumors immediately; letting them build only creates misunderstandings.
7. Be aware of office politics and gossip, but refuse to participate in them. Make it a policy to communicate with all equally as well.

Becoming an Investigator

Once you've listened, you can ask effective questions. Questions do two things: (1) they allow you to discover more information, and (2) they let the speaker know that you were listening. There are five types of questions:
1. Open-ended questions = These encourage discussions. Ex: What do you feel would improve your performance, Don?

2. Closed-ended = These require specific yes/no or one-word responses. Ex: Did you call on Michelle this week?
3. Fact-finding questions = These are aimed at getting more specific information. Ex: What specifically does your activity sheet show as your strengths and weaknesses?
4. Follow-up questions = These types of questions elicit an opinion. Ex: How did you like the way this morning's meeting went?
5. Feedback questions = These are very targeted questions. Ex: Do you think we'll need a closer deadline for this task force project?

Taking Massive Action

Most of all, to make your communications most effective, follow through or ACT on the new information you delivered or received from the communication. Most communications requires a responsive action. Respond to the information you have gathered by listening and taking notes. Keep your promise and let your salespeople know the results and progress of your action to their suggestions or issues. Sometimes the action best taken might be to simply pass on the information. However, be sure to let your salespeople know you have done that.

Communicating from the H E A R T

I believe the most important form of communications is when it comes from the HEART! Here's what I mean by that:

H = **HEAR** what your salespeople tell you are their concerns and questions.
E = **ENTHUSIASTICALLY** promise to consider their suggestions and innovative ideas.
A = **ACT** on your promise—let them know that you are following through.
R = **REINFORCE** your expectations by clearly communicating your expectations and then taking the next step to make sure they are well equipped to exceed your expectations. What is the next step?
T = **TRAIN** yourself and your people to become the best!

Working Through the Process--Chapter Thirteen

❖ What do your salespeople need to know more about your...

Company:

_____

Product:

_____

Customers:

_____

Competition:

_____

Job Responsibilities:

_____

❖ Who is responsible for communicating the necessary information to your salespeople? How can you improve communications?

_____

_____

_____

❖ List four strengths and four areas that need improving in your communications.

Communication Strengths:

1. _____

2. _____

3. _____

4. _____

Areas of Improvement:

1. _____

2. _____

3. _____

4. _____

❖ What are some of the new communication strategies you plan to implement with individuals and your entire sales team?

Individuals:

_____

_____

Team:

_____

_____

❖ Seven Keys to Communicating for Results:
1. _____ playing _____; make _____ feel important.
2. Be _____ and _____ to your people.
3. Set aside time for _____ communication.
4. Remember, _____ disagreement can be _____.
5. Make your purpose known for _____ and _____; _____ agendas can arouse _____.
6. Address false rumors _____; letting them build only creates _____.
7. Be aware of office _____, but refuse to _____.

❖ Write down how you plan to change your current methods in order to communicate with your HEART.

H = HEAR the issues and concerns of your people.

_____

E = ENTHUSIASTICALLY consider their suggestions and innovative ideas.

_____

A = ACT on the great suggestions your people offer.

_____

R = REINFORCE your expectations through clear communications.

_____

T = TRAIN your people to become their best.

_____

CHAPTER FOURTEEN
Managing the Challenges of Change

"The key to the ability to change is a changeless sense of who you are, what you are about and what you value."
                                                    Stephen R. Covey

Chapter Highlights:

▶ Resisting Change

▶ Overcoming the Challenges of Change

▶ What is the Catalyst for Change?

▶ Growing with Change

▶ Knowing What and When to Change

▶ Developing an Action Plan for Change

▶ Training for Change

If there's one thing that's here to stay—it's change. Businesses and their people must change to remain competitive in today's marketplace. So, why not become a trend setter instead of being a trend follower? As Lee Iaccoca would put it, "Lead, follow, or get out of the way!" Leading is ideal—following is necessary—getting out of the way may be impossible when you're talking about change within your sales team. Sometimes that's just not an option—saying "NO" to change may mean saying "NO" to your competitive edge in the marketplace, and your salespeople saying "NO" to their careers. So, there are far-reaching results to saying "YES" to change—to being the first to adopt change.

Marketing and advertising gurus have proven to us that most of the time you don't have to be the best—you just have to be the first, in order to be viewed by others as the best.

> Taking a proactive approach to change TODAY is the only way to take charge of change TOMORROW!

That's what I'll be discussing in this chapter—how to keep an open mind to change and open the doors to endless and ever-expanding opportunities for you and your people.

Resistance to Change

Many mediocre managers are resistant to change. How about you? How do you feel about change? If you are open to change and its challenges, your organization can stay competitive and your people will be given every opportunity to grow in an industry where change is not an option to be considered but a necessity to be welcomed. Teaching yourself and your people to welcome the challenges of change can enrich their careers and personal lives as well. So, what about it? Are you ready to embrace change?

Okay—still hesitant? Well, don't worry if you are—you're in good company. Our industry is filled with managers who don't move forward and neither do their people because they have a difficult time with change. Don't become one of those people. Instead, read this chapter carefully, and study the "Working Through the Process" section in order to teach yourself to overcome and master change.

Dealing with Change

Managers deal with change in one of three ways.
1. Resist
   These are the types of managers whom many call the "sacred cows" of the industry. They like things just as they've always been. They believe what worked well yesterday will also work well today. This is a false security, though.

> Times change, and if you stay focused on yesterday's management methods and sales strategies, you'll be yesterday's news in the marketplace.

Eventually you'll have to give up your resistance and follow the pack.

2. Follow

Most managers who follow the pack were once resisters. At least becoming a follower is a step above not changing at all. Let's look at the position of being a follower. Is that where you really want to be? Do you want your company to follow the innovative ideas of another company and be second in design? Do you want to follow what the manager did before you who may not have been as effective as your superiors would have preferred? Do you want your salespeople to follow behind their competitors?

If the answers to these questions are "NO," then what must you do to avoid putting yourself in that position? Well, you've got to LEAD.

> Being a leader requires taking more chances, but it also means reaping more benefits. Leadership means having more responsibility, but it also means enjoying more control.

So let's look at the managers who lead the way to effective changes.

3. Lead

If you are a manager who leads by way of change, I would venture to say you forge a more adventurous path and are experiencing greater financial rewards than those who resist and follow. There are also some other benefits to being a true leader. Managers who LEAD their people create positive, inspiring environments where there is more job satisfaction and higher morale. Motivation for them is a two-way street. They motivate their salespeople to go out there and exceed the company's expectations, while their people move them to continue to be outstanding managers.

Characteristics of a GREAT Leader

L	They fall in **LOVE** with what they do.
E	They are **ENTHUSIASTIC** about the goal.
A	They have the right **ATTITUDE** about the people they lead.
D	They have the **DISCIPLINE** to learn everything possible about the situation.
E	They **EMULATE** fellow leaders who are greater than they are.
R	They have earned the **RESPECT** of the people who follow them.
S	They revel in the **SUCCESS** of all of their followers.
H	They are **HUMBLE** about their own successes.
I	They rely on their **IMAGINATIONS** to envision the achievement of each goal and their next situation for personal growth.
P	They **PRAISE** in public and criticize in private.

What do you have to change to provide that kind of leadership? Let me ask you—is change a natural thing? You'd certainly think so by all the changes we are asked to make in our lifetimes. However, even for some who embrace the benefits of change and encourage their people to welcome it—change isn't always easy. Sometimes managers don't see the positive affects of change because of the immediate challenges of working through the process before getting to the gains. Few things are more disappointing than putting in all the efforts that change requires, yet having the results be less than expected or a total flop altogether.

Change is a Natural Occurrence

If you look at nature, change IS a natural occurrence. It is the same way with people and organizations. Governments, corporations, family structures, even the changes within ourselves—change plays a huge part of our growth. The same rings true with management. Changing methods and strategies, changing team members, changing skill levels and knowledge bases, changing market demands, changing product lines—see what I mean?

Being great in the sales arena requires more than change—it requires being GOOD at change.

Managers who are leaders have learned to respond positively to the uncertainties of change rather than ignore the necessity of change. They recognize the fact that change brings new opportunities and increased enthusiasm to their people. And, they seek out people on their sales teams who are open to that same philosophy.

Causes of Change

The way I see it, there are three major causes of change.

1. Social Causes
    Social causes include the growth in youth and consumer markets. There has been a great shifting in consumer trends. We have changed from a community-centered society to an individual focused one. We have become the "What's In It For Me" generation of consumers. What does this mean to your salespeople? For one, they greatly influence societal demands, and they, in turn, drive the sales industry. They dictate how your salespeople will sell and who they'll sell to. They determine what needs to be changed, and they predict how long those changes will be effective.

2. Economic Causes
    These changes can be very slow to occur, yet they grab a very powerful stronghold of the public's perception of the marketplace. If your salespeople's customers perceive the market to be in a downswing—then for them it definitely is. Because they believe business to be falling off, they actually predict what they think will occur and produce the predominating culture of their companies. In other words—they believe their business will decrease, therefore, it does. If not contained, these negative predictions can spread from one department to another, from one company to another. Pretty soon, the predictions have become the reality—business is way off and salespeople are suffering. Those are economic predictors or causes of change.

    What does the manager do in a situation like this? He or she definitely needs to change the belief systems and morale of their people. And, they need to create situations where their people will buy into the need for change. Their failure might mean the future well being of the company.

3. Technological Causes

It's very important, as a leader, that you refuse to hide from new technology. Welcome it! The rapid speed of ever-changing technology is having a profound impact on methods of management, customer service, manufacturing, purchasing power and overall sales.

In order to accomplish current tasks more efficiently and to prosper in a competitive market, managers will need to invest the necessary time and money into acquiring the latest technology and learning how to use it. Even though the newest technology may appear irrelevant today— tomorrow it may be indispensable.

Look at computers. Yesterday, they were just for corporate use or perhaps in the production of advertising and print media. Today, almost everybody has an at home computer. My friend's eight-year-old knows how to command and manipulate a computer as well if not better than I do.

Changing Your Perspective on Change

Ever ask yourself why your child accepts and adopts change better than you? There is really a simple answer to that question. Children look at change as positive, exciting stuff. Why? They haven't had all that experience to teach them otherwise. They haven't been laid off due to corporate change. They haven't yet experienced heavy repercussions for some decisions they may have made that brought about a need for change that was resisted and fought against.

Because of these experiences, as adults, and as managers, we tend to value our own protection more than we value the changes that might be wonderful for our company. So what are the sources of change for your company? Most of the sources of change come from within. For instance, you may receive a directive from your superiors that requires change. You may respond to the needs of your salespeople and to be effective—you're facing some pretty extensive changes. Or, you may see market trends and decide on some innovative changes within your sales team or your management style that will make you leaders in the industry. In that case, the source of change was your own personal initiative.

There are two ways to change. You can either adopt change over a long period of time, or be forced to change radically in response to urgent needs of your department or company. Let's take a look at both.

Gradual Change

Gradual changes are usually easier for most people to accept. They occur over a prolonged period of time, and often expand over many departments or are company wide changes. In these situations, your people are given the time they need to adjust to the changes, and they are usually allowed to process the change—to discuss the affects these changes will have on their individual growth. Because of the time that gradual changes allow your people, they often have more ownership and less challenges with these types of changes.

Radical Change

Radical change is another story, altogether. Radical changes are sudden—marked with dramatic side affects and extensive aftermath. Usually radical changes are on a very large scale where the organization or department must stand together in order to gain and prosper or simply survive the change. These are especially difficult to accept when your department or company has experienced great success with the way things used to be. The traditional thinkers want to remain status quo.

This is when you, as the manager, must step in and practice your skills in crisis management. Since radical changes are often implemented to avoid catastrophe, it's your responsibility to share the true picture and possible outcomes with your people. Your management style may drastically change as well during radical changes within your department.

For example; during a crisis, changes are best made by one person or a small group who can act quickly and efficiently. Your team must develop a plan to prevent a pattern of trial ups and downs that can be triggered by a major crisis. But it doesn't have to be totally negative. Look at these times as learning experiences. It's the time for you and your team to develop a proactive attitude rather than a reactive one. It's a great opportunity to grow by leaps and bounds!

Growing with Change

I've stepped into many a management position where the company was struggling with its production and people, and although I saw great possibilities for growth, it also required a great amount of work and changes to bring about that growth. It was fortunate for me that the relationships I had with my people were strong enough to withstand the winds of change. Based on their past successes under my management, they put their trust in me that the next change would be equally as powerful and positive as those they had already experienced with our company. That history of success can be just the jumpstart for change that your team needs.

> I consider growth the payment for embracing change.

No matter if the changes are slow or more radical, or a combination of both, your salespeople will experience change and it's up to you to lead them in the ways that will make those changes easier and more effective. Depending on the changes and the personality types of your people, some will handle changes automatically and other changes will come up against heavy resistance from your salespeople. Why put everybody through difficult changes? Why not just leave the harder stuff until your team is more open to the changes?

Proactive managers cannot afford to wait until all their people welcome change. If they did, positive changes would never happen. There are always going to be a small group of resisters—you can plan on it. Managers, good managers, gain the advantage in the marketplace by changing before others see the need to change. They are first to adopt innovative ideas that will make them "lead dog" in the pack.

Powerful leaders recognize the fact that they can offer their salespeople additional resources through change. They can acquire a broader customer base by changing their product lines or company policies. Perhaps they can decrease product or service costs and enable their salespeople the opportunity to offer exceptional products and services to their customers at a significantly lower cost than their competitors. It could be that by changing their territorial boundaries, your people will have a more expansive distribution with quicker deliveries. And, this is an easy task—but all you've got to do is get your people to accept change! Well, easier said than done, right?

Accepting and Allowing for Change

Learning to accept change is a major change in itself. It's a good idea to adopt an attitude that change means opportunity. This positive attitude will permeate all departments and involve them in the process, which in turn will give your people greater ownership into the change.

In order to ensure all are involved, there must be positives for everyone and the changes must show immediate benefits. It isn't that most of your salespeople are not willing to put up the efforts change requires, but they don't want to do so if it doesn't bring the positive results that were promised.

Knowing When to Change

Other than urgent or radical change, there is a time to change. But, how do you, as a manager, know when that time has come? Customer driven, or external change, is indicated by the systems you have in place now. Many managers choose to use tools like customer surveys to identify the needs of their customers. Others use win/loss reviews or self-evaluation sheets to review situations where business was lost to the competition. Then they question why and determine the necessary changes needed to win next time. Still, other managers know the value of visiting other departments and listening and observing their customer contact to determine changes that need to occur in their sales departments. For example, if customer service communicates a common customer complaint that could be remedied by changes in the sales department, then it's TIME FOR CHANGE!

Then there are the indicators for change within your own sales team. I call these types of changes—internal changes. When morale drops, that is a big indication that change is needed. A good way to get your people to buy into those changes is to involve them in their own solutions. Allow them to make a plan for change.

Falling sales figures also indicate a need for change. It could be more a change on your part than that of your salespeople. Good leaders look to themselves first when these things happen. How about you? Do you need to change your management methods in order to create high-energy salespeople? What can you do differently to stimulate sales and enthusiasm? How will these personal changes on your part affect individual members of your sales team?

What to Change

Once you've determined when change is necessary—it's time to work on the "WHAT!" What needs changing? Don't try to change everything at once—it's too chaotic. Concentrate, instead, on areas where there is the most dissatisfaction. This is when you need to listen to opposing opinions. Listen to your salespeople. Listen to the "problem" cases within your sales team. They can give you the bigger picture.

Before you put major changes into place, look at the boomerang effect these changes may have in other departments and be proactive and preventative in your communications.

 Don't settle for the short-term patch because it's an easier solution right now. It could require a long series of changes down the road that will tire your salespeople and stretch their willingness to work on change.

Who Helps in the Process of Change

When you decide what needs changing, avoid overloading the same people with the responsibility of carrying out the challenges of change. Unfortunately, managers are so busy that when they find those willing to implement changes, they often give them more than they bargained for. As much as you are tempted to do this, I'll warn you it will eventually lead to burnout.

Those who are most involved are those who most benefit. Determine which key

 I mentioned it before, but it bears bringing up again—one of the most important things to remember when undergoing change is to involve everybody in the effort.

people on your team need to buy into the changes first so that they can bring others around. Then solicit their help in developing a plan of action with other influential people on the team. Make sure you reward them along the way for the extra efforts to help you implement the new changes.

Once the changes have been introduced to your key people and the wheels have gone into motion, give your salespeople time to process and discover what these changes will mean to them personally. Empower your key people with decision-making capabilities to carry out their plans. Recognize their successes and share and encourage them when they experience temporary setbacks.

One of the things I've observed in my years of management is that I sometimes expected too much too soon from my people. Set up reasonable expectations rather than creating an atmosphere of frustration. There is a limit to how much change people will accept within a certain time frame.

Stagger and prioritize your changes.

Simple Action Plan for Change

I've spoken about an action plan for change, so what does that entail? First, clearly communicate the purpose for change and the benefits those changes will bring. To get everybody involved, give salespeople responsibility in implementing the changes. Be sure to value their efforts. Support their decisions, both emotionally and by providing additional resources they need to effectively bring about the changes.

Since some people don't take changes well, be flexible in your time frames and your plan of action. If you run up against a great deal of resistance, you may need to reevaluate your changes or give your people a bit more time to implement those changes. It's always a good idea to make a success schedule. Display your team's progress where everybody can witness their efforts, and reward their accomplishments. When positive results come rolling in with your outstanding management of these changes, be sure that those results are posted as well. It's a way to publicly recognize your effectiveness as a manager and your salespeople's willingness to work hard for the betterment of the entire department or company.

Anticipating and Overcoming the Challenges of Change

To minimize disappointments, be sure to prepare your people for what could go wrong. Nobody likes ugly surprises or unexpected events that hinder forward progress. Anticipate what challenges will need to be faced during your implementation phases of change. Then, set the stage for how your team plans to deal with those challenges. Finally, put into place some preventative measures that could head off trouble before it strikes.

Once your plan is in place, the next step is to implement it. This is where training is an absolute must.

Realizing that with change come insecurities and a lack of confidence on the part of your people—training can get them over the hump—through the learning curve.

As with any new process, the time your people are learning the changed system or programs may create some confusion and put some constraints on their time. But, those are the demands during the learning curve.

If you keep your people focused on the long-term positive rewards for implementing these changes, they'll be more willing to suffer the temporary challenges they'll have to overcome. Short-term sacrifice for long-term gain.

The Benefits of Training for Change

As I said before, this is the time that expert training can be motivational and energizing. Change can mean a great deal of added efforts and more time spent on teamwork. Training helps to bring quicker and more effective positive results, which in turn encourages greater participation. Everybody likes to do what brings them success.

There is another even greater benefit of training. It promotes a united commitment to excellence. When you are creating a history of past successes brought about by accepting change, your salespeople will be less hesitant to welcome future changes. When they understand that implementing changes means being flexible when you run into snags in the current system, they won't feel bad when their suggestions need adjusting or modifying.

Suppose the worst happens, and you've established change that just isn't going to work. Your methods and management style should be one that is non-threatening to your people. Create an open learning environment where salespeople feel safe enough to express their opposition to implementation. Welcome that opposition—it may be the key ingredient that saves you a lot of time down the road.

When your people see the benefits of training, it gives them knowledge of how—not just a feeling they're being forced to accept the changes directed by upper management. By effectively communicating how implementation occurred in the past, they see how others worked through similar challenges and came out winners. It doesn't take too long to see the importance of training people in the new skills and strategies changes will require.

> The best thing you can do for your people is to give them the "We can do it" attitude. Before you know it, they'll **be gaining through training.**

Effective training will give your people the success momentum they'll need to carry them through the challenges. Being a great coach will help your people move forward and reach their goals, but make sure you provide follow-up training for the next step of change. Build on one successful implementation of productive change to another one. Train your people to be change engineers.

Working Through the Process--Chapter Fourteen

❖ In the past, how have you resisted or welcomed change? Explain.
Resisted Change:

_____

_____

Welcomed Change:

_____

_____

❖ The Three Major Causes of Change
Social Causes
    1. Growth in _____ and _____ markets.
    2. Shift from _____ centered society to an _____ focused one.
    3. These changes influence _____ demands.

Economic Causes
    1. Can be ____ to occur.
    2. Grab a very _____ stronghold on the _____ perceptions.

Technological Causes
    1. Many companies ____ from it instead of _____ it.
    2. It's rapid changes are having a profound impact on methods of _____, _____ _____, _____, _____ and _____.
    3. Today's managers will need to _____ current tasks more efficiently to survive the changes.
    4. New technology that may appear _____ today may be _____ tomorrow.

❖ How have the three major causes of change affected the need for change in your company?

Social Causes:

_____

Economic Causes:

_____

Technological Causes:

_____

❖ Define Gradual Change vs. Radical Change

Gradual Change
1. Grows _____ over a _____ period.
2. Company wide changes are _____ at a _____ rate.

Economic Causes
1. A _____, _____ change with marked affects.
2. Often this type of change is on a _____ _____.
3. Organizations who _____ _____ will gain most from radical change.
4. When large organizations have had great ____ success, _____ is harder to _____.

❖ What changes do you foresee in the near future? Are they gradual or radical?

1. _____

2. _____

3. _____

4. _____

5. _____

❖ How and when do you plan on implementing the indicated changes?

_____

_____

_____

_____

❖ List three specific ways you plan to get your team to buy into the necessary changes in your department to accommodate the growth of your company.

1. _____

2. _____

3. _____

❖ Knowing that change brings along with it the need for training, how do you plan to train your people to face the challenges of change?

_____

_____

_____

❖ What will be the benefits of that training for you and your team?

_____

_____

_____

CHAPTER FIFTEEN
Make A Stand Against Stress

"Almost means not quite. Not quite means not right. Not right means wrong. Wrong means the opportunity to start again and get it right."
Dan Zadra

Chapter Highlights:

▶ The Effects of Stress
▶ What Does Stress Cost Your Company?
▶ Stress Spillover
▶ Stress Exists--Manage It

L ike bad weeds in a garden, stress can grow in your life until it simply takes over your productiveness and purpose. Although we all live under stress, some still refuse to recognize its overwhelming presence. It feeds on happiness until it eats away at the very fabric of careers and personal lives. What began as a minor annoyance can develop, in no time, to a full-blown battle against an army of negatives.

The Stress Attack

As a manager in today's world, you're getting attacked on all sides. Many suffer stress from superiors, salespeople, family and even self. What about you? Do you often feel like you just want to run away? Do your daydreams consist of escaping to a simpler way of life? Are you calm on the outside, yet raging on the inside? Are you overly forgetful, or unable to be one-minded at work or at home? Do you wish for just one whole, worry-free day?

If these statements fit you, you could be setting up yourself and your family for heartbreak. Throughout this chapter, I'm going to teach you to spot your stress warning signals. You'll learn to identify and overcome stress interference that affects your physical and mental well being.

When Does Stress Occur?

Stress is present any time the body is required to perform beyond its normal range or capacity. Within limits, stress **can** be used to motivate you to achieve. Unfortunately, once on a roll, most managers don't know how to turn off their stress and enjoy. Consequently, the stress of management has "done in" many potentially great leaders who fold under the pressures and demands of today's sales industry. What are the effects of stress on one's physical and emotional condition? Tremendous!

Who Invited Stress, Anyway? What Is It Doing Here?

Stress can significantly increase your heart rate, blood pressure, metabolism and physical activity. Since I know few managers who need more things to do in less time, with more pressures from within to achieve success, I'm not sure just how beneficial even the slightest amount of stress is to becoming an effective leader.

I've made an interesting observation throughout my years in management— what is believed to be true about over-worked managers and their stress levels really doesn't seem to be the case. The amount of work doesn't create the stress—but rather the low levels of sales success. It's not the lack of time that creates stress— but the inefficient management of time. And, it doesn't seem to be over-achievers who suffer stress, but the frustrated under-achiever whose poor management skills and inadequate team-building strategies distance them from their dreams.

 When success eludes you, stress pursues you! Soon, instead of trying to develop your people and manage your team—you're developing health problems and trying to manage your own mental and physical health.

Your focus has now shifted from helping others to succeed to simply helping yourself to survive. What happens then? You're trapped in a vicious cycle of the need to achieve and the need to relieve.

What need do you choose to satisfy first? Most managers would say, "Well, you definitely have to relieve the stress, first. After all, without good health you cannot function as a leader."

> While I agree that good health is a necessary ingredient of effective management, it is the by-product of success. So, if you choose to treat poor health first, you may be treating the symptoms and never eliminating the cause—poor performance.

Therefore, stress builds until it becomes a chronic disease disguised by ongoing symptoms that distract us from attacking its root source.

Prolonged stress not only attacks your physical self, but it can be psychologically devastating. When the pressures of management get too tough, many seek comfort in a drink or two after work, or perhaps a pill at night, just one, to help you sleep. Again, this is not a cure, but a cover-up. Instead of advancing in their positions, these managers retreat into private depressions, disorganization and discouragement. Before long, they find themselves regularly seeking refuge in substances that temporarily alter their state of mind—that allow them to temporarily escape to a better place. Did you know that drug and alcohol abuse costs our country over $100 billion annually? I can tell you, those dollars are not all being spent on recovering teens—it's taking its toll on the professional arena as well.

You may be thinking, "Yeah, but I'm not a drug addict. I live in a nice house and hold down a good job. I'm not hanging out in bars every night or peddling drugs on the street." Let me ask you a question, though. How much work did you miss this year because of poor health? How many times did your doctor prescribe over-the-counter drugs to help you get over that nagging cough, or persistent headaches, stomach ailments, sleeping disorders or nervous conditions? The consumption of prescription drugs has drastically increased because the stress levels have decreased our overall health.

Managers who suffer stress are much more likely to indulge in destructive behavior, and when they do they're not the only ones to suffer. Extreme mood swings can alienate their colleagues and destroy a productive learning environment for their salespeople. While a troubled manager's confidence decreases and his or her depression increases—the salespeople ride that roller-coaster right along with them.

**What Effect Does All This Have on a Company,
Managers and their Salespeople?**

1. Stress creates an inability to make decisions.
    It's almost impossible for stressed out managers to focus on one thing when there are dozens of demands on every moment of their day pulling them in 50 million directions at once. What do you do? That's when you call it quits. STOP and let the world get off!

> You cannot control every situation or circumstance, but what you can control is how you react to them.

Devise ways to alleviate or eliminate your heavy stress. For example, avoid working too many hours or weekends. Delegate more routine tasks. Build in treats to yourself that create your own positives in your scheduled work. Get some physical exercise during the day. Walk at lunch. If your company has an exercise room—use it after an especially stressful day.

Most of all, be one-minded in what you do. When you are at work, focus on successfully doing your job—one activity at a time. Clear your desk of clutter. Hide it in a drawer if necessary, but put one file or one thing on your desk at a time and work on that issue until you have it resolved. Close your door to interruptions if necessary. Make it known to your people that for these two hours every day you will not be available.

> When you clear your schedule and clear your desk, you'll learn to clear your mind and focus on one task at a time.

As you recover from the high stress, you can then go back to balancing several things at once—but, for now, do the one-item management method.

2. <u>Stress causes workers to have conflict that is much more difficult to overcome because of the high emotional baggage</u>.
   If you fear reprisal for poor performance, and that poor performance is constantly reinforced and strengthened by undue stress, inner conflict begins to eat away at a manager's self-esteem and confidence. When this happens, their people may suffer some of the same symptoms. Their sales drop off, and they begin to listen to that unreasonable little voice within that says: "What's the matter with you? You used to be a good salesperson, but you just don't have it anymore!" With all that negative inner talk, comes emotional baggage. And, when you carry the weight of the world on your shoulders—it isn't an environment that encourages great decision-making.

3. <u>Stress causes high levels of absenteeism</u>.
   Obviously, the health problems I've mentioned can cause managers and their people to miss work, but sometimes the emotional challenges a stressed person experiences are much more debilitating. They are also more difficult to treat because they are often hidden under a warm smile and almost overly enthusiastic attitude.

It takes excellent leaders to recognize high stress levels in their people, and even better ones to help eliminate those stresses.

> Just because a salesperson is at the office, doesn't mean they are present.

Some are so down from the pressures and demands of their jobs that they are accomplishing little more than warming the chair. They miss days at a time without ever being out of the office. They forget directives and outcomes to meetings, because all the while they weren't mentally present.

What's even more difficult are managers who cannot help their people because they cannot help themselves. They have all they can handle just trying to cope with their own stress. I hope you've heard that message so far in this chapter.

Don't Forget

You cannot help your people if you haven't taken care of yourself, first!

4. Stress also creates greater staff turnover.
    It's so much easier to blame others for job dissatisfaction or inner
    discontent. You know if frustrated managers do that, so do their people.
    When things get bad and stay that way, people tend to leave rather than
    resolve the problem.

    Instead of a manager being part of the solution, they become a part of
    the problem. Unfortunately, most stress cannot be diminished with a
    30-minute pep talk or even a weekend away. Deep stress, stress that
    has been allowed to fester, may require ongoing treatment. Leaders
    who are equipped to diagnose stress and prescribe treatment usually
    practice some of the following management methods.

    They may meet with the person privately to see if he or she is experiencing
    outside pressures that are affecting performance. If they are, they know
    company services that offer employees the attention they need to see them
    through the crisis. If the pressures are in-house, though, the manager is
    well aware of the things to do to help that person deal with stress rather
    than choosing to leave the company. That's when they recommend some
    of the things I spoke about earlier, like exercise and suggestions that will
    help them to cut their hours by working smarter instead of harder.
    Effective managers know what motivates their people. They know their
    personal and career goals. Once those things are discovered, the rest is a
    matter of reminding them of those goals and asking how they can help
    them with their commitment to achieve. Management is just as much a
    people business, if not more, than is the salespeople's experiences. And,
    great managers take the success of their salespeople seriously.

5. Stress in the workplace can also cause poor customer relations.
    After all, when you have unanswered concerns within yourself, who
    wants to address the complaints of another? Because stressed people
    become so inner focused, it's difficult for them to listen to and care
    about the problems of their customers.

    When managers or their salespeople are on the edge of stress, they react
    instead of respond. They impatiently jump to conclusions about what
    it will take to please the customer, and in doing so, they fail to resolve
    the problem. Instead of customers knowing how much your people

care, they question that any caring exists at all because of the salesperson's inability to deal with even the slightest conflict.

What can be done? Besides all those things mentioned above like exercise, open discussions with management, creating a non-judging, safe work environment for your people—the best thing you can do is to let your salespeople process and freely express their feelings and beliefs. Encourage them to confront their stress and discover ways to relieve it. Remind them of their goals and what it will feel like to achieve them. Help them to extend their vision outside of their stressed inner-self and put themselves in the customer's space.

6. Stress can also bring about a decrease in safety records.
When your salespeople are unable to focus, many safety issues become involved. For example, if it is necessary that they travel a territory and they cannot keep their mind on driving, your people may suffer more accidents. If, during the course of a demonstration, your salespeople are required to operate any kind of machinery, safety issues may also be compromised due to stress. All these things, plus a general lack of rest and concentration because of added stress tend to create safety concerns.

7. Lastly, stress can create poor quality control.
If your people are stressed because they must meet quotas, they just might be met at the expense of product quality. Many corners are cut by stressed people. They tend to be less detail oriented and more willing to be satisfied with inferior product. Either the salespeople recognize products and services need improving but don't care, or they simply aren't focused enough to notice. Either way, stress can greatly interfere with product and service quality.

Recognizing the Monkey on Your Back—STRESS!

How do you know if you are stressed or not? This may sound like a crazy question. It stands to reason that those suffering stress should be able to feel the tension, right? Well, not necessarily. We are quite flexible, really—able to adjust to one higher level of stress piled upon another. What happens is that we become accustomed to dealing at a higher stress level until we get comfortable at that level.

The next thing you know, your stress increases yet again, and again our minds and bodies fool us into believing that we're not really THAT stressed.

One way to measure your stress is to keep a stress journal. You'll discover times in the day, the week or the month where you tend to be more stressed than at other times. It could be due to something as simple as your food intake that regulates your energy levels is not sufficient. Or, your stress could be caused by something as complex as monthly reports or weekly sales meetings.

Whatever the cause, analyze your ability to cope with the unexpected challenges. Are you throwing up your arms and feeling as though you just can't cope? Worst yet, are you doing this right in the middle of what, at one time, you would have considered to be only a minor upset?

Stress has a way of doing that—making it increasingly impossible to deal with things that would have only before been a slight interruption in our day. It's a buildup of stress—and it continues to build until you begin to feel as though you're about to blow!

Another way you'll know if you are stressed is if you continually experience a feeling of being trapped. Are you emotionally tight? Do you feel as though you are right in the middle of one giant panic attack? Tension from stress can give you that "fight or flight" feeling.

Speaking of flight—many people under great stress feel like withdrawing instead of attacking. The more stress they experience, the more they sink into the corner of a sales meeting, refusing to offer their input and contribute to the team's effort. Do these behaviors sound familiar?

What are High Stress Levels Costing Your Company?

1. Less quality and more customer service concerns
2. More complaints and dissatisfied staff
3. High staff turnover—more money in training
4. More money in marketing and recruiting
5. Even your good reputation

Stress Spillover

If you are under a considerable amount of stress at work, it won't be long before you're showing the symptoms in your personal life as well. It's a well-known fact that more and more managers are taking stress home with them. Let me ask you a question, how eager are you to go home and make stimulating conversation after a stressful day at work?

Managers communicate all day long. They are in meetings, giving directives, reviewing concerns with an individual salesperson, problem-solving with upper management, and the list goes on and on. They carry on heavy communications all day long. The last thing managers want to do when they get home is have debates with their children or discussions with their spouses. No! Tops on most manager's list when they get home is vegging in front of the boob tube and giving their mind a rest.

Because many managers withdraw behind a curtain of stress, there are many more tensions in the home. Their marriages can't stand the stress. What happens then—managers allow the stress to negatively impact their marriages and divorce rates begin to soar.

One stress stacks on top of another, and soon the manager is looking for an outlet. I'll ask you—what gives us more comfort than eating? A side-product of stress in many people is eating and sleeping disorders.

Extreme stress causes us to behave in the extremes.

We either eat too little or too much. We sleep too few hours, or we let stress make us sleep around the clock. All this added stress can cause some severe secondary health problems in managers and their people.

When all these things heap on top of the shoulders of your workers, they begin to experience an overall dislike of their station in life. They don't like themselves, their jobs or their personal situations. They don't have enough money, time or personal freedom. Since many people who are stressed have an inability to focus on solutions, all they do is counterproductive to finding a solution. They focus on the lack in their lives instead of the positive possibilities.

What You Focus on and Give Thought to Becomes Your Reality

A friend of mine once told a fellow salesperson after having an especially productive quarter that he just COULDN'T BELIEVE the last month he had, but he was going to enjoy it while it lasted. "Numbers like those only come around once in a lifetime," he commented.   Then he shook his head with a smirk and continued with the conversation.   In fact, if I heard him make that statement once, I bet I heard it a dozen times.   Over and over again, my friend was unintentionally reinforcing negative sales results.   Well, guess what eventually happened?   He predicted his own failure!   He never again posted those kinds of figures within a 90-day period—and I imagine he found his mediocre results to be quite BELIEVABLE.

I tell you this story because I believed the self-talk and thoughts of my friend created the very thing he feared would happen.   All he could think about and talk about was how UNBELIEVABLE those figures were.   He gave it so much thought that its power grew and grew until he accurately predicted the outcome of every quarter that followed.   Finally, he became what he BELIEVED himself to be—a poor producer.

Don't get me wrong!   I'm not suggesting that you ignore stress in your life. That would be an impossible request, wouldn't it?   Rather, what I'm suggesting is that you learn to identify your stress, treat it and work to overcome it in both your workplace and personal life.

Being as close to my family as I am, I've always depended on them to keep me balanced and less stressed.   We plan together as a family to play as hard as we work.   That way, when I have one of those weeks when everything gets to me, I look forward to the great times I'll spend with my family and friends.   I make appointments with my family just as if they were my prospective customers. Although I love my career, my #1 priority is my family.   And, I can't make them my focus if I'm stressed out about work and feeling guilty that I'm not working when I'm spending time with them.

What about you?   Are you enjoying what you are doing right at this moment?   Why not?   Are you making the mistake of postponing your happiness until you achieve this or experience that?   You know what?   Don't wish you were at home when you are working, and worry about work when you are at home. Enjoy what you are doing at the time—and make the best use of every moment.

Who Are You Kidding?

Stop trying to convince yourself that you are just not going to let stress affect you.   That's pretty unrealistic.   Instead, I'd ask you to learn from this book and its stories.   Knowledge can be a great stress reducer.   We know that knowledge is power, and applied knowledge is even more powerful.   Success can almost wipe out stress altogether.   Why?

Success changes your focus. You're no longer concentrating on what you don't want to happen but rather on what you love about your job.

You're looking at what you want to continue to experience.

The next time you're tempted to let the stresses overtake the joys of your day, think twice about what you could be missing. You could be missing opportunities to lead your people to greater achievement. You could be missing higher year-end profits. You could be missing the personal rewards of success. I don't know about you—but I don't intend to miss out on a moment of fun and excitement that a successful career in sales can offer.

Congratulations

I wanted to congratulate you for reading this book. It is a great stress reducer. If you commit yourself to adopting its principles, you'll reduce your stress and love your work. Customers will notice the change in your people, and your people will notice the changes in your management style. Suddenly, instead of your focus being turned within—you'll be able to listen to your people's concerns with true interest and empathy.

Working Through the Process--Chapter Fifteen

❖ What is currently interfering with your mental and physical well being on the job and creating undue stress?

_____

_____

_____

❖ How has this stress affected you and your salespeople?

You:

_____

_____

Your Team:

_____

_____

❖ List five things you can do to alleviate or eliminate your stress.

1. _____

2. _____

3. _____

4. _____

5. _____

❖ What are high stress levels costing your company in the areas of...?
Product Quality:

_____

Closed Sales:

_____

Employee Satisfaction:

_____

Marketing and Recruiting:

_____

Reputation:

_____

❖ How is your stress at work spilling over into your personal life? What will
you do to minimize its negative results?

_____

_____

_____

❖ One of the best stress reduction methods is to love what you do--DO YOU
LOVE YOUR WORK?   What can be done to create more enjoyment and
FUN in your work? Your personal life?

Work:

_____

_____

Personal Life:

_____

_____

CHAPTER SIXTEEN
In Pursuit of Greatness

"Many of us spend our lives searching for success when it is usually so close that we can reach out and touch it.
Russell H. Conwell

Chapter Highlights:

▶ Commit to Greatness
▶ Take the Test to Learn the Lesson
▶ Forming New Habits
▶ Adopting the "I CAN" Attitude
▶ REAL Principle of Success
▶ The Rewards of Pursuing Greatness

W hy do I call this chapter "In Pursuit of Greatness?" In today's market, if you want to be an outstanding manager, you must actively pursue greatness. I'm sure you've heard the saying "Opportunity knocks but once." Well, I say, "Why wait for opportunity to come knocking?" Instead of waiting for opportunity to find you, you be the hunter and flush out opportunity.

That's the problem with many managers and their people. If they set their mind on one achievement, and the outcome was less than what they'd hoped for, they keep struggling with the same old pursuit instead of changing their picture of greatness. The wonderful thing about pursuing greatness is that if one behavior or belief doesn't work—it isn't written in stone that you must pursue 'til the death. Give it up and hunt for greater opportunities in different areas.

You're Charting Your Own Course—And, the Map Isn't Drawn in Blood

Like I said, if one opportunity doesn't have the results you desire, seek another direction. There's one thing about opportunity, it comes in many forms. Sometimes opportunity can be disguised as a problem, when it is really an opportunity to learn. At other times, opportunity can step back and hide around the corner of a great challenge. However, the only way for us to reach and take full advantage of the opportunity is to first be strengthened by conquering the challenge. Being flexible is the key to greatness.

We all know the story of Michael Jordan. There have been few, maybe none, who have achieved what he has achieved in basketball. In fact, many believed Michael had reached the top in performance—and the problem was, so did Michael. When he adopted this belief system, what did he do? He quit! There were no other challenges for him to conquer. So, he changed sports—he pursued greatness in baseball. Ah, but just because Michael Jordan was an outstanding basketball player, he quickly learned this was not a guarantee that he could be an outstanding pro baseball player.

Now, Michael could have continued playing baseball, but instead he tapped that flexible, positive attitude of his. He got REAL—RECOGNIZED his "real" talent; ELIMINATED the negatives he was hearing or telling himself that he couldn't make it in baseball and now he couldn't go back to being the king of basketball. He moved back into basketball, practiced and ACQUIRED a renewed spirit, a new desire to achieve in that sport. Lastly, he LAUGHED at himself. He didn't consider what he did to be a mistake—it was an experience. Later on in this chapter I'll be teaching you how to get REAL with yourself and your people.

A Commitment to Greatness

That's where commitment comes into play. If you commit yourself to doing whatever it takes to grow into a great manager—then how can you fail? If you are willing to study other greats in the sales management and selling industry and encourage your people to do the same—then how can either you or your team fail? Well, believe it or not—you can.

Although studying is very important, knowledge isn't enough to make you great. You can know what every great manager has done before you when faced with a similar problem, but unless you apply that knowledge—you're not going to improve as a manager.

> You must work harder on yourself than you do on your job to become a great leading manager. That's called job security.

Make yourself more valuable, and the more valuable you become the more value you create in the marketplace. The power of knowledge comes in its application.

Your ACTIONS need to reflect your increased knowledge. In other words, if you previously had a management style of control and demand, but now know that you and your people will have far better results if you change your management style to one of encouragement and empowerment—know this: it's going to take a little time.

Forming New Habits

It will take time for you to form new habits and get a few successes under your belt. And, it will take time for your people to accept the new you, without harboring disbelieve or mistaken judgment. You see, both you and your team have been conditioned to things as they've always been. Allowing yourself time to adjust, giving yourself permission to make mistakes, then discovering the positive possibilities of change can be an incredible <u>undertaking</u>. If you're not careful—it can <u>take</u> you <u>under</u>!

Take the Test to Learn the Lesson

Don't be afraid to take the test to learn the lesson. Ask yourself, "Am I willing to pay the price to become the best?" Believe me, there is always payment—always an exchange of positives and negatives. For instance, if you have decided that you need to build a more productive, effective team, then your test might be the question of whether you are willing to invest in professional training for both your team and yourself as their coach. After you and your team have learned the new skills, the next test might be to empower them to become decision-makers. I believe this next point to be the toughest test of all—get out of the way of your people. Very difficult commitment to make when you're used to having total control.

Looking for a Mentor or Role Model

Sometimes it's good to look outside the sales arena. There are many courageous and committed individuals who have forged the way for your greatness. From them, you can learn that anything is possible. It could be that you are a dedicated sports fan, admiring those who have devoted their lives to the physical and mental challenges of the game. You sure don't have to look too far in that field for a mentor for greatness, do you? I mean, if Tiger Woods could succeed when his youth and race presented its own set of challenges on the golf course, you can surely find the courage to pick yourself up during the tough times managing your team, can't you? If Tiger can learn from life's challenges—what about you? Can you take the test to learn the lesson?

Adopting the "I CAN" Attitude of Success

Maybe it's the arts you admire—film celebrities and television stars. Well, if a young man, recognized for his youthfulness and good looks, his talent as an actor, Michael J. Fox, can confront his fears, go on national talk shows and appear on the cover of *People Magazine*, openly admitting that he is in the advanced stages of Parkinson's Disease, don't you think you can confront your fears and move your team to greatness? You can!

If a princess can give her life to the fight against poverty, hunger, and bring unity and peace to the world, don't you think you can develop that same unity within your organization? You can! But, once again, you need to be willing to pay the price—to take the test. Believe that you are capable of becoming a great leader, and you will be. Expect greatness from yourself before you demand it from others.

Your Personal Vision of Greatness

What is your own personal definition of greatness? Well, let's see. Does one of these statements sound like you when you're considering what it will take for you to feel as though you're successful:

1. WHEN I become a millionaire, THEN I will think of myself as successful.
2. WHEN I have led my team to doubling its sales, THEN I will think of myself as a great manager.
3. WHEN I am promoted, THEN I will feel as though I have the power to change things.

If these statements sound like you—I'd say you're suffering the WHEN—THEN mentality. Give up the WHEN—THEN thinking. You may not realize it, but thinking this way is making you postpone your greatness. Instead of pursuing it—you're waiting for it. Instead of enjoying the journey—you're waiting to reach your destination before you allow yourself the celebration of success.

I'll tell you a secret—okay, it really isn't a secret. Many of you have heard this statement many times, but for some reason it didn't get from your head into your heart. Success comes in the small victories you'll experience during your journey to greatness. If you don't enjoy the journey, you may have an awfully long wait for greatness. And, your ability to sustain may be compromised because you haven't allowed yourself time to enjoy—to celebrate.

Let me give you a new perspective on greatness—it's what I do best. Every one of you reading this book is well on your way to achieving greatness. As you read the book you are in pursuit of greatness. You thought enough of yourself and your people to invest in the education and knowledge it will take to become a great manager, and you can pass that on to others. I think that's GREAT!

You're Already Great—You Just Don't Know it Yet

Like I said, every one of you is GREAT. You've worked hard, picked yourself up when things beat you down and remained focused on your goal to be a great manager. If that really wasn't a goal, consider yourself to be great anyway. You have accepted the challenge of management. You are now establishing your criteria for greatness and moving in that direction.

What is the criteria for greatness? If I could answer that one, you couldn't afford to own this book. I can tell you that it is different for everyone. The criteria for greatness is your own private test—your own step-by-step changes that make you a better person and, consequently, a better manager. I can tell you that there are, as I see it, four steps to take before your journey to greatness—I spoke of them earlier. They spell out the word REAL—and I like to use them because they give

REAL meaning to leadership—REAL difficult challenges to overcome in order to reach greatness—REAL pleasure and enjoyment in celebrating your success.

Let me share with you my **REAL** principle.

R = RECOGNIZE the fact that there is work to do in preparation for your journey toward greatness. Work harder on yourself than you do with your people, in order to become the best.

E = ELIMINATE negative thoughts that keep you from greatness. Get that negative voice within you under control. When it tries to rob you of your opportunity to achieve greatness—refuse to believe it; take away its power.

A = ACQUIRE an unbeatable positive attitude. For some of you, this will be one of the most difficult things to do. Managers in today's markets take a lot of abuse—it's up to you to create the positives in your day. Plan for them. Discover what it takes to make you happy, and plan on experiencing those things. Schedule them in your day timer. If it makes you happy to watch your son's little league games, schedule them in your days. If it gives you happiness in your life to go out to lunch with a friend, plan to do that this week. Just as you plan on your day's productivity—you also have to plan for your day's positives.

L = LAUGHTER is one of the greatest tools to building your success as a manager. First of all, learn to laugh at yourself. Believe me, you aren't the first to have done something completely stupid—and thank goodness most of the dumb things we do aren't recorded in history books or seen by millions on CNN. So next time your behavior warrants it—have yourself a good laugh!

Negativity and depression just can't live where there is laughter. Do a little experiment with me. Wherever you are right now, I want you to smile. Some of you have felt the pressures of management for so long, you could be taking a chance that your face will crack under the pressure. Take the chance. Whether you're in your car, walking with your headphones, or just reading this book while you are locked away in your office—SMILE.

First a little smile—that's good. Now let yourself chuckle. For some that's a real crackup, just a little chuckle. Think of a really funny time you experienced with your family, your children, your significant other, and let yourself laugh out loud. Give it a good laugh—one from the belly. Now, get mad—feel negative. Can't do it, can you? It's just impossible to feel those feelings when you've given yourself permission to laugh. I'm a great believer in laughter. It's one of the strongest weapons against the negatives we have, yet few people use it to chase the negative from your office, your conference room, your car—or even within your minds. Don't let the pressures of management make you forget how to LAUGH.

So that's how I prepare people for their journeys to greatness—get REAL. But, it still isn't easy. The pursuit of greatness carries with it some pretty heavy sacrifices.

1. TIME = When others are watching their favorite television programs or going out with friends, you may need to beg off for the evening in order to work to be a better manager.

2. RISK = The pursuit of greatness will always be accompanied by the risk of failure. After all, you don't have to worry about failure if you never push yourself beyond your perceived limits. What is worse, though, is that you'll be left to wonder what could have been, if only . . . I hate playing the "IF ONLY" game. If only I had taken the time to become a better leader. If only I had anticipated that challenge before it hit our salespeople. The thing about the "IF ONLY" game is that it can go on forever and nobody wins.

3. MONEY = The pursuit of greatness also requires you to invest money in your development. Like you did when you invested in this book, or that last cassette series you bought, or that seminar you are considering attending. When the investment comes out of your pocket, you can think of a million other things to spend it on, can't you? The thing about investing money in your management training and education is that it can offer you incredible returns. So, rather than thinking that you are spending the money—think of it as a loan to yourself. You're going to collect great interest rates and high dividends.

4. CHANGE = When you pursue greatness, you are moving out of what is familiar and comfortable and moving into the unknown. You really

don't KNOW that you will achieve your goals; you are simply in pursuit of them. That uncomfortable place is what imprisons many people in their pursuit. They listen to the negatives and give up their dreams of greatness. So, expect change—welcome the challenges of change. But also, expect to experience discomfort with the changes. After all, it's not comfortable to put yourself out there and admit you've made mistakes that you'd like to begin to change. It's not comfortable to try new things and worry if they'll work, or wonder if your people will buy into the new you. But discomfort is short-term.

5. ISOLATION = Sorry to say it, but the pursuit of greatness may mean you grow beyond your buddies and other co-workers because you are moving toward greatness and they may be lulled by contentment. They may not see the necessity to strive to become the best. In the process, you lose your common ground. The benefits are there though when you make new friends who are riding the same elevator to greatness.

6. FAILURE = I can guarantee you that you will experience temporary setbacks as you move to greatness. Your success will depend on what you do with those failures—how you react to them. Do you cover yourself with a sheet of pity, or arm yourself with the shield of passionate involvement in your work? It's your decision.

Just like any other changes you are in the process of making, although those changes come with some challenges—they also come with rewards. Let me give you an example: "When I was just a scrawny kid, I had a burning desire to be strong—fast—powerful. Now, I could have looked at the bigger young men in my class and listened to that inner voice say, "How can you even think of being more powerful than them? You are so little. Look at how powerful they are. Why, they're built for speed. They're the winners in life."

Instead, I chose to listen to my father as I worked with him in the garage he built behind our house, after leaving his business in Cuba when Castro's regime challenged the very principles my father lived by. He could have given up and I would have had a much different life. Instead, he took his test—learned the lesson. It was so difficult for him. He was a proud, successful businessman in Cuba, but change required that he leave all that behind and become dependent on others for food and shelter in a country where he knew no one and couldn't speak the language.

My father reached out and found greatness. He was willing to pay the price for greatness. As I worked with my father and shared with him my doubts about becoming as strong as some of the boys in my class, or as fast and powerful as they were, my father told me stories about where I came from—about what kind of men were in my family. He told me they were the strongest, most powerful men in Cuba. They were the most determined, most courageous, most clever people in the country. Little by little, the words my father spoke began to take root in my mind, in my heart. And, that year, in 8th grade, I believed myself capable of achieving whatever I wanted. I worked out until I could lift more weight than anyone in my class. I ran track and imagined myself a winner until I actually began taking first place at almost every meet. My father helped me to have the pride and inner strength that it took to overcome my perceived shortcomings.

I know that not all of you have had the advantage of a father like mine, but nobody is left to walk alone in his or her pursuit of greatness. And, just like I imagined myself a winner, so can you. Like my father, if you are willing to do whatever it takes in your pursuit of greatness, there will be endless rewards to claim along the way. What are some of those rewards? Well, let's take a look at people who are in pursuit of greatness and examine their rewards.

The Rewards of Going After GREATNESS

- CONFIDENCE = One success leads to another. When you accomplish your first success in your pursuit of greatness, you often have doubts that you'll be able to duplicate the process. Soon another success follows and then another. Before you know it, your repeated successes begin to give you the confidence that you are on your way to experiencing greatness.

- ATTRACTION = As you get further into your pursuit of greatness and get several successes under your belt, you won't believe the people you'll begin to attract into your life. You see, greatness attracts others who are in pursuit of their greatness as well.

Have you ever noticed how those who achieve greatness are surrounded by other achievers? That's no accident—it's by design.

Miserable people feel very uncomfortable around those in pursuit of greatness, so they are attracted to other people who have given up the journey. It's difficult for negative to thrive within when your thoughts and actions are crowded with the positive. And, positive is like a magnet—it just draws to it more powerful positive.

- INCREASED ABILITY = Once you achieve, those achievements bring you greater ability to continue to achieve. Why? Well, for one, your belief system changes. Once I won a race on my track team, and I knew what winning felt like, I began to have a desire within me to win, which eventually overcame my fear of failure. Once I won, it was easier for me to believe I could win again. I refused to let myself believe that my performance was just a fluke, or that my opponent just had a bad day. Instead, I choose to believe that my ability to win was a direct response to my preparation. It was up to me. If I were willing to change my beliefs and behavior, there was no reason I couldn't continue to come in first.

- ACHIEVEMENT OF YOUR DREAMS = When you maintain constant pursuit of greatness, it isn't long before you realize that you can accomplish today what was only a dream yesterday. And, you allow yourself to dream bigger, to picture greater achievements. So, your personal picture of greatness changes. It gets broader—broad enough to reach out to all those around you—just like my father.

Not only are you rewarded, but those you manage will reap the rewards as well. Why do you think people want to be around a winner? Your ability to become a great manager changes their opportunity to become great salespeople. Greatness has a way of rubbing off on everyone with whom it comes into contact.

You're Not In this Alone

Let's face it, no matter how great a manager you are, you can't do it alone, can you? It takes a team of people in pursuit of greatness to make your efforts successful. If you, as a manager, are perceived and believed to be one of the best managers in the company, don't you think your superiors recognize the fact that you didn't get there alone. You have a GREAT team.

If you are attempting to reach greatness all by yourself, you're missing the whole idea of success.

 Success is richer and more enjoyable when there are others there with you to share the experience. Everybody wants to be a part of a winning team.

I have mentored many managers, and not once have any reached greatness alone.

I find that managers who have the easiest time recruiting, usually do because salespeople have heard how great it is to work on their team. Top producers didn't get where they are because they gave all their power away to a controlling manager who wanted to take credit for his or her people's personal growth and achievements. No!

 People who are empowered—have power. Managers who encourage—have courage.

Teams who achieve—perceive themselves to be a productive, important ingredient to the entire team.

Greatness—A Constant Pursuit

The wonderful benefit of being in constant pursuit of greatness is that the pursuit is constant. Reaching one destination just makes you want to move forward to another. Once you reach your personal picture of greatness, the picture changes and you're off again. Greatness has a way of spreading into other areas of your life, too.

When you've reached greatness in your career, pretty soon you'll find you are involving yourself in a GREAT relationship. When you've reached greatness in a relationship, you may then pursue reaching greatness in parenting. Pursuing greatness at work allows you to expand your thinking to recognize that you want to pursue greatness in your recreational life as well.

You can use the same principles to achieve greatness in every walk of life. The more you change, the easier change becomes. The more you are willing to pay the price, the smaller the price becomes. What began at the cost of great sacrifice and effort, will improve with practice.

Once you've won the first time and conquered your mistaken beliefs, the winning becomes that much easier. Now you can focus on what you want because you have a clearer vision of greatness. It doesn't seem so far out there—and you don't feel so removed from success. Most greats will tell you that success is built one recovered setback, one reinforced goal and one achievement at a time.

I welcome your feedback. On the last page of this book, you'll find our office address and contact numbers. Let us know how you and your people have benefited from our program. If you have any suggestions for my next book, I'd welcome those as well. I always want to be open for innovative ideas and creative leadership strategies. As I mentioned before, I believe in order to continue to be a great teacher, I must never stop being a good student.

By reading this book, you too have come one step closer to assuming your proper leadership role. You have taken an important step in raising the level of your achievement by reading these pages, and I want to take a moment to express my appreciation for your efforts. Congratulations for recognizing the importance of strong training to help you learn all the great things you're capable of achieving. It's proactive and progressive leaders like you who are changing the face of our industry. It's caring and communicative leaders like you who are listening to the needs of their people and discovering ways to bring added professionalism into the marketplace. Most of all, it's open-minded leaders like you who have made my lifelong goal of becoming an effective educator a worthwhile one. May your quest for success be rewarding and fulfilling. I wish you great success! God Bless!

Working Through the Process--Chapter Sixteen

❖ What is your own personal definition of greatness?

_____

_____

_____

❖ How do you plan on achieving greatness in your career?

_____

_____

_____

❖ Moving toward greatness, what challenges do you expect to encounter along the way in the following areas?

Time:

_____

Risks:

_____

Money:

_____

Change:

_____

Personal Growth:

_____

Exposure to Possible Failures:

_____

❖ Since success is in the journey, what rewards will greatness bring you along the way?

_____

_____

_____

❖ What about your people? How will reaching greatness influence greater levels of performance on their parts?

_____

_____

_____

❖ How will reaching greatness in your work spill over to the following:

Relationships:

_____

Lifestyle:

_____

Personal Achievements:

_____

Parenting:

_____

Inner Strength:

_____

❖ What Can You Do To Become A GREAT Leader?

G = GENERATE _____ and high _____ in your sales team by _____ what you do and letting it show.

R = READ and _____ other great management _____ and _____ that would be effective to _____ with your team of professionals.

E = EMPOWER your people by clearly _____ you and your company's EXPECTATIONS to provide _____ and _____ to your salespeople's efforts and _____ their creative responses.

A = Promote an ATTITUDE that is _____, _____ and _____ for ALL.

T = TRAIN _____ and your _____ to become their best!

INDEX

INSURING CONTINUED SUCCESS...

Since learning is an ongoing experience, I encourage you to continue your quest for success by investing in yourself and your business. Here's how...

❖ Request our catalog of audio, CD and video programs designed to reinforce fundamentals and introduce innovative strategies that establish you as the recognized expert in your field. Make them an important piece to your business library.

❖ Inquire about my national and international public appearances, custom seminars and 2 and 3 day workshops, corporate presentations and ongoing training programs. My assistant will be happy to send you a schedule, additional information, or contact you in person to address your specific needs.

❖ Send your questions, observations, and personal accounts that occurred as a result of reading this book and adopting its principles on leadership. Who knows, perhaps you'll be a contributor to my next book.

OMAR PERIU

Omar Periu conducts sales training and motivational seminars nationally and internationally, specializing in:

- Sales Training
- Sales Management Training
- Inspirational/Motivational Seminars
- Conventions
- Coaching and Mentoring Programs
- Audio, CD, Video Cassettes

If you want your next meeting or convention to be a guaranteed success and leave a lasting impression on your people, call or write for more information or a free product catalog:

Omar Periu International, Inc.
P.O. Box 812470
Boca Raton, FL 33481
888-777-4519
e-mail: OPeriu@aol.com
www.OmarPeriu.com

To continue your personal and professional development, you will want to acquire more of *Omar Periu's Success* materials

1. SALES LEADERSHIP PROGRAM

For over a decade Omar Periu has been known as the leading sales management authority. Mr. Periu has trained over two-thirds of the Fortune 500 sales managers. This program will teach you the qualities of superior leadership and how to manage yourself and others to obtain peak performance. Learn to set and achieve your sales goals, improve your delegation and leadership skills, assemble a team with the "right stuff," and develop high impact, motivational techniques. (8 audio cassettes / 16 sessions with interactive manual)

2. INVESTIGATIVE SELLING AUDIO

Make the income you deserve! All sales masters understand and use these proven secrets of "Investigative Selling." In this 16-session, thought-provoking, audio program, Omar will teach you how to overcome fear, find and qualify clients, make dynamic presentations and dramatically increase your sales-closing ratio. (8 audio cassettes with interactive workbook)

3. INVESTIGATIVE SELLING BOOK

Discover in this best-selling, "how to" book, the proven skills that will make your career skyrocket. Omar will teach you what he and countless other top producers and business owners know—how to turn "No's" into "Yes's." You'll learn the 12 Principles of Investigative Selling that made Omar a self-made multi-millionaire by the age of 31. This book is a must for any serious student of selling.

4. AWAKEN THE WINNER WITHIN AUDIO

Omar Periu is synonymous with success. As a non-English speaking immigrant, Omar overcame the odds and created a life that most people only dream about. He knows what it takes to develop the success-building desire—a desire so intense and complete that it leads you to the secrets of greatness. (6 audio cassettes / 12 sessions)

5. HOW TO MASTER THE ART OF EFFECTIVE TIME MANAGEMENT

All highly paid sales executives know how to manage their time, their lives and their territories. In fact, effective time management is one of the highest paid skills in the world. In this audio series, Omar will teach you how to create a time-management plan that will work as hard as you do. He'll also teach you to organize, prioritize, overcome procrastination and set goals. Keep your career on track with effective time-management skills. (6 audio cassettes / 12 sessions).

6. DEVELOPING POWER PROSPECTING STRATEGIES TO GET IN

Learn how to prospect anyone, anywhere, anytime. Omar Periu is a successful public speaker, author, business owner, sales executive, writer, recording star, performer and, above all, an exceptional teacher. He has made a lifetime career of helping people bring out the very best in themselves, their families, organizations and communities. In this program, he will share with you the tools to become a champion prospector, a master at phone strategies—both hot and cold calling techniques. You'll learn effective networking strategies to build your business prospecting from the bottom up and get through back doors to the top VIPS's of Fortune 500 companies. Experience how Omar will help you achieve success and greatness! (6 audio cassettes / 12 sessions)

7. THE POWER OF MOTIVATION

How To Develop and Maintain A Positive Mental Attitude will help you to build a better self, team and company through effective and innovative techniques. In this compelling program, Omar shares with you his "how-to" ideas and proven principles that have enabled him to become a multi-millionaire. He presents inspiring stories and motivational concepts that will help you maximize you and your team's future success. Upon completion of the program, you'll be encouraged to face your fears and kick your counter-productive habits. Enjoy the benefits of becoming a calculated risk taker; think about where you are now, where you want to be and how to reach success as quickly as possible. This is the ultimate, instruction course that will empower you and your people to handle rejection, remain slump-free, and capture the lion's share of the marketplace. (8 audio cassettes / 16 sessions)

8. HEALTH IS WEALTH – HOW TO HAVE THE ENERGY TO SUCCEED

By taking control of your life choices and learning how to master your habits, you can embark on your journey to personal fulfillment! Learn how to increase your capacity for stress by recapturing your energy. This program will be your tool to reaching new mental, physical and emotional heights. You'll soon realize the importance of your daily decisions and how they impact your personal power to achieve top fitness. (6 audio cassettes / 12 sessions)

9. PREMEDITATED SUCCESS AUDIO

Premeditated Success, a simple-minded guide to health, wealth and happiness. Omar will share with you the "how-to" principles that were taught to him by his mentor, Tom Murphy. Omar Periu and millions of others live a life in fearless pursuit of their dreams because of this outstanding goal-setting system created by Omar and his mentor, Tom. (8 cassettes / 16 sessions and interactive workbook)

10.HOW TO RAISE HAPPY, HEALTHY AND SUCCESSFUL KIDS

This is a program designed to help parents discover the special skills that will help their child succeed in life. Learn what you can do to make your child a winner! A must for parents and grandparents who want to play an active role in helping their children develop healthy self-images, build family unity, nurture self-discipline, and rise above life's negative influences. (6 audio cassettes / 12 sessions)

**Call for Additional Information or a Free Product Catalog
Omar Periu International • P.O. Box 812470
Boca Raton, FL 33481 • 1-888-777-4519**